CAMBRIDGE
UNIVERSITY PRESS

Narrative

Marcello Giovanelli

Series Editors: Dan Clayton and Marcello Giovanelli

CAMBRIDGE
UNIVERSITY PRESS

University Printing House, Cambridge CB2 8BS, United Kingdom

One Liberty Plaza, 20th Floor, New York, NY 10006, USA

477 Williamstown Road, Port Melbourne, VIC 3207, Australia

314–321, 3rd Floor, Plot 3, Splendor Forum, Jasola District Centre, New Delhi – 110025, India

79 Anson Road, #06–04/06, Singapore 079906

Cambridge University Press is part of the University of Cambridge.

It furthers the University's mission by disseminating knowledge in the pursuit of education, learning and research at the highest international levels of excellence.

www.cambridge.org
Information on this title: www.cambridge.org/9781108402293

© Cambridge University Press 2018

First published 2018

20 19 18 17 16 15 14 13 12 11 10 9 8 7 6 5 4 3 2 1

Printed in Malaysia by Vivar Printing

A catalogue record for this publication is available from the British Library

ISBN 978-1-108-40229-3 Paperback

Contents

Series introduction

Cambridge Topics in English Language is a series of accessible introductory study guides to major scholarly topics in the fields of English language and linguistics. These books have been designed for use by students at advanced level and beyond and provide detailed overviews of each topic together with the latest research in the field so as to provide a clear introduction that is both practical and up to date.

In all of the books in this series, we have drawn on examples of spoken and written language. We hope these will encourage you to apply the theories, concepts and methods that you will learn in the books to analyse data and to think critically about a number of issues and debates relating to language in use. Many of the books also draw on data from the Cambridge Corpus. Throughout each book, you will find short activities to help develop reading and writing skills, longer extended activities and practice questions that will enable you to explore your learning in more detail and research findings that will provide inspiration for your own language investigations. Each of the chapters includes suggested wider reading, and a full glossary and reference section at the end of each book will support you to extend your learning and provide avenues for future reading and research.

We hope that each book will give you a good overview of its topic and, that taken as a whole, the series will map out some of the most interesting and diverse areas of language study, providing you with fresh thinking and new ideas as you embark on your studies.

Dan Clayton

Marcello Giovanelli

How to use this book

Throughout this book you will notice recurring features that are designed to help your learning. Here is a brief overview of what you'll find.

Coverage list

A short list of what you will learn in each chapter.

KEY TERM

Definitions of important terms to help your understanding of the topic.

ACTIVITY

A clearly defined task to help you apply what you've learnt.

RESEARCH QUESTION

A longer task to help you go deeper into the topic.

PRACTICE QUESTION

To give you some practice of questions you might encounter in the exam.

Ideas and answers

Further information, suggestions and answers to all activities and practice questions in the book.

Wider reading

Key texts to help extend your learning.

Topic introduction

This is a book about stories. In the five chapters that follow, you will explore the kinds of stories we tell and how we tell them. You will explore texts from a range of modes, genres and periods that have been written for a number of different audiences and purposes. Together, these show just how central stories are to human beings and how we use them to structure our experiences and create meanings for our listeners and readers.

Chapter 1 provides an overview of narrative, drawing a distinction between story content and the ways in which that material is shaped in communication. Chapters 2 and 3 develop this discussion by providing more detailed explorations of written and spoken narratives. In Chapter 4, the focus shifts to examining how readers position themselves in relation to narratives and how they make connections between different kinds of reading experiences. Finally, Chapter 5 examines three specific narrative genres: hard news stories; narratives spoken and written by children; and the narratives created on the social media platform Twitter. For all of the chapters I have provided wider reading suggestions that will extend your understanding and that I hope you will find useful.

The best way, of course, to understand how narratives work is to explore them using the ideas, concepts and methods introduced and mapped out in each of the chapters. This book therefore encourages you through activities and research tasks to find and examine your own examples. Stories are everywhere and I hope this book enables you to generate and explore data of your own!

Marcello Giovanelli

Chapter 1
Defining narrative

In this chapter you will:

- Explore ways in which you can define and classify the elements of a narrative

- Understand the concept of representation as a fundamental part of narrative

- Examine the strategies writers and speakers use to make narratives interesting and relevant to others

1.1 Some basics

1.1.1 Telling stories

This chapter will outline some fundamental principles behind narrative and introduce some preliminary ideas and definitions that will be developed in subsequent chapters. Our starting point is the fact that storytelling is a core human phenomenon: we tell stories to babies and young children, we watch stories on TV and in films, we talk to our family and friends about what we've done, our interests and our hopes and desires for the future, we categorise memories into stories that we have captured on film or in photographs and store them in albums. We enjoy finding out about other people's lives either by reading about them in magazines and autobiographies or following them on social media. And, of course, we are also interested in stories about fictional people, evident in the popularity of reading literature as a pastime. Put simply, stories are everywhere.

In fact, reading stories has been demonstrated to have significant benefits. The psychologist Keith Oatley has dedicated much of his academic career to showing how reading fiction is a kind of simulation in so far as readers play out emotions, feelings and dilemmas in a virtual environment as a way of developing knowledge and skills that they can then use in the real world (Oatley 1999). And recent research in cognitive psychology has shown that reading fiction can improve empathetic skills. For example, a study by Raymond Mar and Keith Oatley (2008) showed that regular readers of fiction tended to have greater social skills and that these skills were closely linked to the type of fiction – literary rather than non-literary – that individuals chose to read.

Our passion for storytelling follows a basic human preference for finding patterns and establishing coherence. In fact our minds are naturally predisposed towards creating stories and to organising experiences of events, people, time and places into structures that we then relate for various purposes to various audiences and in various forms.

You can see an example of this tendency by looking at Figure 1.1.

It's quite difficult to describe this image without developing a story frame as a way of explaining what can be seen in it. For example, even a simple description such as 'A man was cycling along a road' provides a starting point for a story. This could be developed by adding more specific detail in terms of time and place, 'One evening, a man was cycling along a road lined by trees', or by shifting the focus of attention to describe the location rather than the cyclist, for example, 'There was a road covered in orange leaves'.

Figure 1.1: Man cycling

In all of these examples, the viewer is, of course, making choices both about *what* information they select and about *how* they choose to present that information. For example, look at the following reworkings of the original description.

'The man was cycling along a road.'

In this example, the indefinite article 'a' has been replaced with the definite article 'the' to introduce the noun 'man'. The definite article tends to be used when the person or thing following it is known or has been mentioned before and consequently can be mentally retrieved by the reader. In this instance, using 'The man' assumes that the reader knows to whom 'The man' refers.

'A man was cycling away from me along a road.'

In this example, the addition of 'away from me' positions the movement of the cyclist in relation to the speaker. The speaker's vantage point in this instance is perceived as being different to that of the original description.

'A man cycles along a road.'

In this example, there is a shift in tense, from the past progressive 'was cycling' to the present 'cycles'. This shift positions the time of telling as the same time as the time of action. As in the previous examples, this subtle difference is crucial to how a reader might interpret the unfolding of the story.

1.1.2 From stories to narratives

The examples above demonstrate how writers and speakers can choose how they want to sequence information, the particular events they want to highlight or downplay, and the ways that they position themselves in relation to those events and the characters involved in them.

So far, however, the term 'story' has been used rather loosely to refer both to the content and the telling. In fact, in examining the *what* and the *how* of storytelling, we have begun to explore the constituent elements of a narrative. We can now define narrative in terms of both its contents and how a narrator presents these to a narratee.

The narratologist Porter Abbott (2008) suggests that the elements of a narrative can be labelled as the story (the content) and narrative discourse (the presentation of that content in the way that it is narrated). In examining the story, we will be concerned with aspects like the plot, characters and the settings in which action and events occur. In examining narrative discourse, we will be interested in the specific choices a narrator has made in presenting the story. This means that we will be concerned with the following kinds of features:

- specific word (lexical) choices

- specific ways in which phrases, clauses and sentences (grammar) are organised

- specific ways in which texts are organised in terms of their layout (graphology) and larger structure (discourse).

KEY TERMS

Narrative: writing or speech that presents a series of events, characters and places in a coherent form

Narrator: a person responsible for writing or speaking a narrative

Narratee: the person to whom a narrative is told

Story: the building blocks of a narrative in terms of events, entities, time and setting

Narrative discourse: the shaping and presentation of the story through choices in language and structure

We will return to these aspects in section 1.2.1 when we explore the important concept of representation.

Figure 1.2 shows how the elements of story can be examined in more detail. In particular, an interesting distinction can be made between constituent events (main and important to the overall story in terms of driving the plot forwards) or supplementary events (not integral to the plot). It is interesting, and important, to note that since supplementary events are not strictly necessary plot-wise, their inclusion will suggest that the author or narrator has a strong reason for including them in the narrative. In other words, supplementary events are frequently used to foreground important ideas, themes or concepts. For example, read Text 1A, an extract from Peter Benchley's novel *Jaws*. In this extract, three men, Brody, Quint and Hooper, have been trying to kill a shark that has been terrorising a community. Hooper is in a cage in the water when the shark attacks him.

KEY TERMS

Constituent events: main events that are crucial to the direction of the story

Supplementary events: secondary events that are not necessarily crucial to the overall story but are included and therefore foregrounded

---

Figure 1.2: Story and narrative discourse

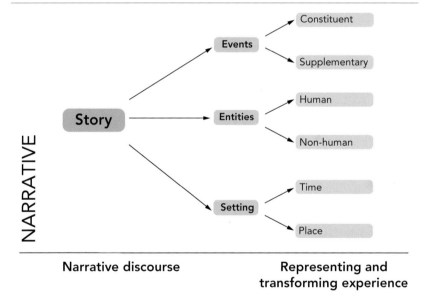

NARRATIVE

Narrative discourse — Representing and transforming experience

---

Text 1A

The fish rammed through the space between the bars, spreading them still farther with each thrust of its tail. Hooper, flattened against the back of the cage, saw the mouth reaching, straining for him. He remembered the power head, and he tried to lower his right arm and grab it. The fish thrust again, and Hooper saw with the terror of doom that the mouth was going to reach him.

The jaws closed around his torso. Hooper felt a terrible pressure, as if his guts were being compacted. He jabbed his fist into the black eye. The fish bit down, and the last thing Hooper saw before he died was the eye gazing at him through a cloud of his own blood.

'He's got him!' cried Brody. 'Do something!'

'The man is dead,' Quint said.

'How do you know? We may be able to save him.'

'He is dead.'

Holding Hooper in its mouth, the fish backed out of the cage. It sank a few feet, chewing, swallowing the viscera that were squeezed into its gullet. Then it shuddered and thrust forward with its tail, driving itself and prey upward in the water.

'He's coming up!' said Brody.

'Grab the rifle!' Quint cocked his hand for the throw.

The fish broke water fifteen feet from the boat, surging upward in a shower of spray. Hooper's body protruded from each side of the mouth, head and arms hanging limply down one side, knees, calves, and feet from the other.

In the few seconds while the fish was clear of the water, Brody thought he saw Hooper's glazed, dead eyes staring open through his face mask. As if in contempt and triumph, the fish hung suspended for an instant, challenging mortal vengeance.

Extract from *Jaws*, Peter Benchley, Bantam (1974)

This extract details one of the constituent events of the novel, Hooper's death, framed by another, the search for the killer shark. Benchley could have simply presented this event before moving on to the climax of the men's fight at sea. However, the final paragraph outlines a supplementary event, the shark returning with Hooper's body in its mouth. This in itself is not a significant event plot-wise and adds very little to the overall narrative. In the context of this extract, however, this telling of this event has substantial narrative power, foregrounding the power of the shark, its ability to kill and the dangers that Brody and Quint now face (Quint later dies trying to kill the shark). Benchley's presentation of the shark celebrating Hooper's death, together with the explicit view that Brody has of Hooper in the shark's mouth, is a deliberate narrative ploy to highlight the helplessness of the men and an example of how authors can add and shape supplementary events for particular interpretative effects.

ACTIVITY 1.1

Constituent and supplementary events

To explore constituent and supplementary events in more detail, look at narratives based on real-life events and people. These might include newspaper accounts of important events such as 9/11 and the film-industry's representations of historical figures and movements such as Laurence Olivier's *Henry V* (1944) and Steven Spielberg's *Lincoln* (2012). You could also explore film versions of novels; for example, *Frankenstein* (James Whale, 1931), *Jaws* (Steven Spielberg, 1975), *Shutter Island* (Martin Scorsese, 2010) and *The Shining* (Stanley Kubrick, 1980).

Do these accounts give additional prominence to supplementary events as well as constituent ones? In the case of films based on books, are there supplementary events that are developed beyond that of the original written version? It may also be the case that some constituent events in the original sources are reshaped when adapted for the screen. Why might this be? For example, in the film version of *Jaws*, Hooper survives.

1.2 Representation

1.2.1 What is representation?

As you saw in section 1.1, the way speakers and writers choose to present material can be as important as the content itself. In fact, all language is representational in that it offers a version of reality that is filtered through the voice of a writer or speaker who chooses to present situations, events and characters in a particular way. For example, in describing Figure 1.1 the choice of 'the man' over 'a man' signalled that the writer was expecting greater reader familiarity with the individual.

Representation can therefore be understood as a process of selection: a speaker or writer selects aspects of the scene that they want to show their audience and presents them in a certain way. For example, look at Figures 1.3 and 1.4. These are images (or representations) of London and they convey very different messages. In Figure 1.3, the image presents London in an unflattering way by showing a street covered in rubbish; the representation of the city in this example is a negative one. In contrast, the clean streets and bright blue sky together with the iconic Tower Bridge in the background in Figure 1.4 provides a very different representation of the city, this time clearly a very positive one. In each case, the reader-viewer is being positioned to share this perspective on the city.

Narrative

Figure 1.3: 'Dirty' London

Figure 1.4: 'Clean' London

Since there is no direct access to reality, the words a speaker or writer uses are always a form of mediation, imposing their way of seeing things onto another reader or listener and encouraging them to share a particular perspective. As the linguist Paul Baker (2014: 73) puts it, representation is 'the creation of a mental image of something using signifying practices and symbolic systems (i.e. through language)'.

A good example of how representation works at the level of language can be seen when you examine the verbal representation of a particular event. Look at Figure 1.5. This is an image that was captured in the Manchester riots in 2011. In this instance, a rioter is throwing objects in an attempt to smash a shop window.

Figure 1.5: Rioter smashing window

Imagine that a news journalist has witnessed and is reporting on this event. There are several choices available to the journalist in representing the scene. At a very basic level, the use of 'rioter' over 'man' is in itself a representational choice that signifies an attitude towards the individual carrying out the action. The event in its entirety might be represented in one of these four ways:

1   The rioter smashed the shop window.

2   The shop window was smashed by the rioter.

3   The shop window was smashed.

4   The smashed shop window.

In each instance, a different aspect of the event is grammatically foregrounded. In example 1, the use of the active voice places emphasis on the rioter. In example 2, the use of the passive voice shifts attention to the shop window itself, which is now the subject of the clause.

A useful analogy is to think of the rioter and shop window on a theatrical stage where the reporter can shine a spotlight on either one to show that it is prominent. In these two examples, the active voice highlights the rioter and the passive voice highlights the shop window. In fact the use of the passive voice acts to defocus the rioter: visually, example 2 places the rioter on the edge of the stage and out of focus. Indeed the passive voice can be used without mentioning the rioter at all, as in example 3. In this instance the rioter is not 'onstage' at all and the reader is unaware of who is responsible for the action. Alternatively, the event can be reported through a noun phrase as in example 4 that simply tells the state of the shop window and offers no indication as to how it became smashed. In this example, the event itself is sidelined; the lack of any verb shifts the spotlight completely away from whoever might be responsible for the action.

KEY TERMS

Active voice: the form where the agent is placed in the subject position in the clause for prominence

Passive voice: the form where the agent is omitted or placed later in the clause

Defocus: the effect of drawing attention away from the agent through the use of the passive voice

---

You will return to the use of the active and passive voice in Chapter 5 when you examine narratives associated with the media and news reporting in more detail. However, it should be clear from this brief discussion that there is a range of options available in reporting on the smashed shop window and that each choice presents a significantly different representation of the same event.

1.2.2 Discourse

So far, you have focused on the representation of events and scenes. In this section, you will focus exclusively on the representation of groups of people and how these representations can be seen as forming larger narratives that promote a particular world-view.

The linguist James Paul Gee (2015) argues that we are exposed to, critique and use a number of Discourses (he uses the term with a capital 'D' to differentiate it from other uses of the term in linguistics) in our everyday lives. Gee defines a Discourse as a way of 'behaving, interacting, valuing, thinking, believing, speaking, and often reading and writing' (2015: 4). Since these actions all involve selecting words and other structures to represent the world, a Discourse is effectively a way of understanding, constructing and acting out the world as one believes it ought to be.

Gee argues that we often use particular Discourses as a result of the various social groups we belong to, the kinds of activities we carry out in our everyday lives and the belief systems that we hold dear, for example politically, ideologically, morally. Each of these belief systems influences the way that we see the world and what we view as counting 'as a "normal" person and the "right" ways to think, feel and behave' (Gee 2015: 5).

Discourse: a way of thinking and speaking about the world, informed by personal beliefs and group membership and ideologies

An example of a particular Discourse in action can be seen in Text 1B, the cover of a popular UK health magazine for men.

Text 1B

Cover of Men's Health, September 2017

This magazine has a fairly defined readership, catering for a target audience which is largely male, generally interested in health and acquiring a good physique and keen to find out about and follow narratives that provide details of how to gain a certain look. Consequently it is part of an overall Discourse (in Gee's terms) that is concerned with thinking about and valuing health and especially physical appearance and what makes an individual (and specifically a male) content. Those who buy this magazine are therefore likely to identify themselves with and 'buy into' this particular Discourse. The acceptance and use

1

of the Discourse itself is therefore one of the defining features of the readership. Indeed, the striking, centrally positioned image of the celebrity actor Ryan Reynolds acts as a visual anchor for the text that surrounds it.

In terms of the text's language, the values associated with the lifestyle the magazine promotes, and with which its readers define themselves in relation to, are clear. Word choices such as 'energy', 'body plan' 'ripped', 'upgrade', 'bigger', 'fastest' and 'regain' are positively-oriented and offer a representation of being a man that is outlined in more detail in the narratives inside the magazine. The cover also has a series of headlines with two prominent and interesting grammatical structures. First, there is the way that noun phrases are presented:

positive or hyperbolic modifier(s) + head noun

'endless energy'
'bigger biceps'
'XL arms'
'lean summer muscle'

Second, these phrase form part of larger clauses:

imperative verb + noun phrase outlining some aspect of health, physique or lifestyle

'lose your gut'
'try our fastest ever body plan'
'upgrade your life'

Together these features exemplify a Discourse of living that includes a perspective on how men should look, a particular attitude towards a certain kind of physique, what it means to be attractive and so on. This Discourse underpins the many articles and stories that appear in the magazine in ways that support the belief systems of those who both produce and read the magazine. These articles and stories in turn are characterised by their distinctive patterns, and in the case of the headlines about them, can be seen to adhere to clear ways in gender is represented.

1.2.3 Subjective and objective narration

This chapter has focused on how a narrative is defined by its overall shape as well as its inherent story. You have explored how the ways that speakers and writers view the world may influence both how material is mediated and the positions and perspectives that readers are encouraged to adopt.

Of course, a narrator can vary the level of more explicit mediation in a narrative by drawing more or less attention to the narrative voice. For example, look at Text 1C, an extract from a conversation involving two family members.

Text 1C

A: You know I think I saw Edward getting off the train one night.

B: He has a job now.

A: Oh he does? Okay cause I saw him up there. I thought I saw him. I said he looks familiar but I couldn't... I wasn't sure.

Cambridge Spoken Corpus

This extract conveys a simple narrative involving Edward getting off the train. It is, however, framed in such a way that Speaker A draws attention to herself, in this instance as much if not more so than Edward himself. Again, using the analogy of the theatrical stage, you can see that Speaker A uses words and phrases that show a level of certainty towards the narrative event, 'I think I saw', 'I thought I saw him', 'I couldn't... I wasn't sure', and which place her *onstage* as a focus of attention as much as the event itself. This subjective narration is common when a speaker wishes to draw to some aspect of their attitude towards the narrative event. In contrast, an objective narration would simply narrate the event without reference to the narrator, who remains *offstage*. In reality, narratives are rarely completely subjective or objective and it is best to think of these as two ends of a continuum. Narrators will tend to use varying degrees of subjectivity or objectivity depending on how they want to present their material and their own stance towards the events they are narrating.

KEY TERMS

Subjective narration: narration where the narrator self-references so as to draw attention to themselves as much as the events of the narrative

Objective narration: narration that is relatively free from any self-reference by the narrator

ACTIVITY 1.2

Exploring representation

Read Text 1D, an extract from an opinion article by Abi Wilkinson that appeared in a UK newspaper. Wilkinson is discussing the aftermath of the UK's referendum in 2016 on leaving the European Union (EU). In this article, Wilkinson examines the idea that one of the reasons voters may have voted to leave the EU was their dissatisfaction with the establishment.

1 Narrative

Text 1D

What if the leave camp actually had a point? Not about quitting the EU, I hasten to add. Though I believe reform is urgently necessary, I'm still convinced we're better off in than out. Nor about the downsides of freedom of movement (wage depression in some industries and increased competition for housing and public services), all of which government policy could counteract, and tax revenues from migrant workers would help fund. Certainly, not about £350m-a-week for the National Health Service or our ability to leave the EU without any sort of economic hit.

But that stuff about smug, out-of-touch metropolitan elites? I can't help but wonder if there was something in that. It's easy to scoff when the line is trotted out by MPs, peers and billionaire business magnates, but they're not really the point. That's just one faction of the ruling class cynically managing to marshal anti-elite sentiment against those on the other side of the argument. The interesting question is why the accusation landed with the public.

'Sick and tired of sending out cash to the rest of the country so they can whine about London and the immigrants who made it for them,' tweeted Ian Dunt, a broadly left-leaning journalist, yesterday.

Was this sweeping, insulting generalisation intended to parody attacks on migrant workers? Apparently not. According to this view the massive wealth, investment and opportunity gap between London and the rest of the country isn't an injustice that needs fixing – rather, people living in leave-voting areas are ingrates who should be happy just to receive "our" scraps. (Where non-London remain voters are supposed to fit into this analysis isn't clear, maybe they're the grateful peasants who should be held as an example to the rebels.)

Extract from 'Leave voters are not all idiots – some Londoners still don't get it', Abi Wilkinson (The Guardian, 14 February 2017)

1.3 The social aspect of narrative

1.3.1 Language as a social tool

The focus so far in this chapter has been on how writers and speakers shape events into a coherent narrative. That is, the concern has been with the overall form of a narrative rather than with its function. However, as you saw earlier in the chapter, humans have a natural predisposition to narrate and the stories we read and talk about can have positive effects on us in terms of developing social and communicative skills. More generally, since humans are essentially social beings, narratives – as with all language – plays an important role in developing our relationships with others. For example, the linguist Daniel L. Everett (2013) believes that language is fundamentally a tool that is used in the establishing and maintenance of social bonds. Ultimately, and from an evolutionary perspective, language is essential to survive! Equally, developmental psychologists such as Michael Tomasello (2003) have argued that language is the vehicle through which young children are introduced and adhere to norms of social behaviour that allow them in turn to interact with others and become full, participating members of society.

In short, narratives are important social tools since we draw on them in our interactions with other people. We can use narratives for a range of social reasons: to collaborate, to persuade and influence, to entertain, to argue, and so on. One of the important consequences of looking at narratives in this way is to acknowledge that narrators themselves have specific functions as they narrate. For example, a comedian telling a joke positions himself in a particular role, as does a teacher talking to a class, as does a police officer speaking to a suspect. In all of these situations, the kind of narrator an individual is depends on the role that they are asked to undertake. Being a narrator therefore naturally results in the projection of a particular self towards others. Indeed a commonly held idea is that language itself is a kind of performance in which we present a version of ourselves to others through the things that we say: the comedian is literally performing on stage but also performing an identity to and for others.

One final interesting example of a particular type of social narrative is the autobiography, a genre where the narrator reframes their own past experiences in the 'here' and 'now'. In doing so, they are not only projecting an identity for themselves but also enacting a specific relationship with their readers. Generally people buy autobiographies because they are interested in the person who wrote them and believe that they provide an accurate and informative portrayal of the individual's life. In these instances, the narrative functions to maintain and enhance this relationship so that we come away from reading an autobiography with what we perceive is a greater understanding of the author's life. In fact the relationship between the different selves of real-life person, author and narrator on show here is complex; this will be explored in more detail in Chapter 2.

1.3.2 Tellability

To maintain the focus on autobiography, read Text 1E, an extract from the beginning of *What You See is What You Get* (2010), an autobiography written by the British businessman and television celebrity, Alan Sugar.

Text 1E

There are three reasons why you might never have got the opportunity to read this book. The first is that maybe I wasn't planned to be in this world, the second is that once I did arrive I was abandoned, and that the third is that my mum – accidentally – nearly killed me! Being twelve years younger than my closest sibling sisters, I often joke that I think (well, I'm sure) I was a 'mistake' – maybe the result of a good night out during the post-war euphoria.

In the late forties, it was normal for babies to be left outside shops in their prams while the mothers went inside. That in itself gives you a picture of what times were like back then – parents were not worried about weirdoes abducting babies. One day, my mum (who hadn't had a baby to think about for twelve years) went to Woolworths and parked me outside in my pram. She did her shopping, walked out and took the 106 bus from Stoke Newington back to Clapton. Only when she was halfway home did it dawn on her: 'I've left Alan outside Woolworths!'

Extract from *What You See is What You Get*, Alan Sugar, Pan (2010)

An important question relates to why narrators decide to narrate in the first place as well as to what it is exactly that makes their narrative interesting. In Text 1E, Sugar is writing about himself and, as a famous individual, assumes that people buying the book will want to know about his life. In this instance, Sugar has the benefit of having a ready-made audience willing to read what he has to say but he also has to make the content interesting and worthy of a reader's attention. He does this through his conversational style, his entertaining opening and his choice of content: the time when, as a baby, he was left outside a shop by his mother. The event itself is a highly dramatic moment that nearly ended in disaster. As such, it has what is termed high tellability.

> **KEY TERM**
>
> **High tellability:** a feature of a narrative whose events are interesting and which has a strong and identifiable purpose

The sociolinguist William Labov (1972) argued that any narrative has its own sense of value to a potential audience and that this value was measured in terms of how relevant and interesting it might be. Labov coined the term tellability to identify the features of a narrative that make it worth telling and, consequently, encourage an audience to invest their time into listening to or reading it. Tellability can be viewed as a continuum: at one end, highly tellable narratives are those that have interesting events and a strong and identifiable purpose. At the other end, a narrative with low tellability will have events that are of little real interest and are uninspiring. For example, in Text 1F, an extract from a speaker talking about a holiday visiting the Grand Canyon in the United States, the likely high tellability of the narrative results from the speaker talking about visiting a location that has a reputation for being interesting and worth visiting, from his description of the activities he carried out there such as seeing the edge of the canyon from a helicopter and from his own evaluations ('the feeling as amazing', 'it was an amazing experience') that present his experience in an appealing way.

KEY TERMS

Tellability: the features of a story that make it worth telling to an audience

Low tellability: a feature of a narrative whose events would be of little real interest to a listener

Text 1F

> Okay so some years ago I went to the Grand Canyon in er the United States and I flew over it in a helicopter. Er I was at the front seat er of the helicopter and the floor was made of er glass so when we'd reached the edge of the Canyon er I could see all the way through down and it was a long way down so so the feeling was amazing. Er we flew around for a couple of hours er next to the cliffs and the rocks and you could see the whole part that part of the Canyon so it was an amazing experience and that I will never forget.

Cambridge Spoken Corpus

Narratives with high tellability may also capture the public's imagination. For example, in May 2016, the English football club Leicester City made history by winning their first Premier League title. This was a remarkable feat given that the team had narrowly avoided relegation the previous season with largely the same squad and were competing, on a modest budget, against more famous and financially powerful clubs. The 'Leicester story' was played out in the media as a triumph of the smaller team and generally interested members of the public, regardless of whether they were football fans or not. Equally, in February 2017,

Narrative

the American Football team The New England Patriots created a dramatic, and highly tellable, narrative of their own when they reversed a 25-point deficit to win the National Football League championship 34–28 in the first-ever 'Super Bowl' to go to overtime. In sport, these kinds of events make for very tellable narratives.

Clearly what might be highly tellable to one individual might have low tellability for another. The notion of tellability is also dependent on the situation of communication, an idea you will return to in Chapter 3. However, often tellability can be measured in terms of the extent to which the contents of a narrative present situations that are dramatic and make us want to read on. In Text 1E, had Sugar's second paragraph simply recounted his mother visiting Woolworths with him as a baby, a reader might be tempted to ask 'So what?' In contrast, the leaving of a young baby in a pram deviates from what readers might expect to happen; it's not the case that mothers leave their children outside shops on a regular basis. The 'lost child' narrative that Sugar narrates dramatises the unusual, and very tellable, event of a child's safety being in danger; this is why, for example, a child going missing is seen as a newsworthy item that receives a great deal of coverage on television, print news and on social media.

A highly tellable narrative can also be particularly deviant in some respects to the point that a reader or listener is compelled to both accept it as highly tellable and question the point of the narrative. Read Text 1G, an extract from the opening to the Italo Calvino short story 'The man who shouted Teresa'.

Text 1G

I stepped off the pavement, walked backwards a few paces looking up, and, from the middle of the street, brought my hands to my mouth to make a megaphone, and shouted toward the top stories of the block: 'Teresa!'

My shadow took fright at the moon and huddled at my feet.

Someone walked by. Again I shouted: 'Teresa!' The man came up to me and said: 'If you do not shout louder she will not hear you. Let's both try. So: count to three, on three we shout together.' And he said: 'One, two, three.' And we both yelled, 'Tereeeesaaa!'

A small group of friends passing by on their way back from the theatre or the café saw us calling out. They said: 'Come on, we will give you a shout too.' And they joined us in the middle of the street and the first man said one to three and then everybody together shouted, 'Te-reee-saaa!'

Somebody else came by and joined us; a quarter of an hour later there were a whole bunch of us, twenty almost. And every now and then somebody new came along.

Extract from *The man who shouted Teresa*, Italo Calvino, Vintage (1996)

The tellability of this narrative rests in its unusual and rather puzzling series of events. The reader wants to find out who the man is and what he's doing, why the others join him, who Teresa is, and so on. It transpires that these questions are never resolved. The story ends with the narrator admitting that he doesn't know Teresa or even who lives in the block of flats. He eventually walks away, leaving a by now large crowd of bemused people with a final stubborn individual still shouting Teresa. The tellability of this story is therefore a consequence of its deviance from narrative norms. With no narrative resolution or logic to the narrator's actions, readers have to assume a set of reasons as to why the story was written in the first place. In fact, it is precisely this reason why 'The man who shouted Teresa' is often read as an allegory critiquing fascism in Italy during the time around the Second World War.

ACTIVITY 1.3
Exploring tellability
Read Text 1H, an extract from a conversation between two friends. Speaker A is talking about memories from his childhood. What do you think makes this narrative tellable? How does the narrator shape and present his story?

Text 1H

A: Most of my childhood memories is just me and my dad. Just riding around with my dad. Sometimes he'd like go undercover and I'd like sit down the block in his car and like watch him.

B: No kidding?

A: Yeah. Go on ride alongs with the police officers.

B: Oh yeah?

A: Go camping with my dad. Stuff like that.

B: Has your dad been involved in any big things that have been on the news or anything?

A: Um

B: Any major?

A: Quite a few years ago you know. Just like he was in San Francisco they like arrested like I think it was like eighty-five motorbikers

Cambridge Spoken Corpus

RESEARCH QUESTION

Tellability

Examine the tellability of sport narratives in the media. You could explore narratives about great sporting upsets, comebacks or about sporting events that have been deemed to be 'great'. How are these presented in various forms and how is their tellability emphasised? As a starting point, you could look at:

- boxing events such as 'The Rumble in the Jungle' (Muhammad Ali v George Foreman in 1974) and 'The Thrilla in Manila' (Muhammad Ali v Joe Frazier in 1975)

- great team comebacks such as 'Botham's Ashes' (England v Australia in 1981)

- significant individual achievements such as the American sprinter Allyson Felix who is the only female track and field athlete to win six Olympic gold medals.

The UK newspaper *The Guardian* has a series (available online: www.cambridge.org/links/escnar6001) called 'The forgotten story of…' that tells the story of various sporting individuals, teams and achievements from across the world. You might also find one of these a source of an interesting narrative. How does the writer make the story being told memorable and worthy of being read?

Wider reading

You can find out more about the topics in this chapter by reading the following:

The structure and elements of narrative

Abbott, H.P. (2008) *The Cambridge Introduction to Narrative* (Second edition). Cambridge: Cambridge University Press.

Gottschall, J. (2013) *The Storytelling Animal: How Stories Make Us Human*. New York, NY: Mariner Books.

Yorke, J. (2013) *Into the Woods: How Stories Work and Why We Tell Them*. London: Penguin.

The website run by Keith Oatley, Raymond Mar and their associates is a useful source of information about their own and others' research in narrative studies: www.onfiction.ca

Representation

Baker, P. (2014) *Using Corpora to Analyse Data*. London: Bloomsbury.

Gee, J. P. (2015) *Social Linguistics and Literacies: Ideology in Discourses* (Fifth edition). New York, NY: Routledge.

Tellability

Baroni, R. (2013) 'Tellability' in *The Living Handbook of Narratology*: http://wikis.sub.uni-hamburg.de/lhn/index.php/Tellability

Chapter 2
Written narratives

In this chapter you will:

- Explore how to distinguish between levels of telling in narratives

- Examine how point of view operates in written texts

- Explore some of the narrative conventions of advertisements and graphic narratives

2.1 Authors and narrators

2.1.1 Levels of telling

Chapter 1 highlighted how the relationship between the author and narrator is a potentially complex one. In this section, this relationship is explored in more detail, highlighting a distinction that can be made between different levels of telling within a narrative.

Read Text 2A, part of the extract from Alan Sugar's autobiography that was discussed in the previous chapter.

Text 2A

In the late forties, it was normal for babies to be left outside shops in their prams while the mothers went inside. That in itself gives you a picture of what times were like back then – parents were not worried about weirdoes abducting babies. One day, my mum (who hadn't had a baby to think about for twelve years) went to Woolworths and parked me outside in my pram. She did her shopping, walked out and took the 106 bus from Stoke Newington back to Clapton. Only when she was halfway home did it dawn on her: 'I've left Alan outside Woolworths!'

Extract from *What You See is What You Get*, Alan Sugar, Pan (2010)

In this text, it would be fairly straightforward for most readers to equate the narrating 'I' with the author, Alan Sugar. A strong connection between the author and narrator is, of course, the hallmark of the autobiography genre. In other forms and genres this may also be the reader's default assumption. Indeed the linguist Elena Semino (1995) has argued that poetry readers tend to associate the 'I' of the poem with the poet. In other genres, however, this connection can be problematic. For example, read Text 2B, an extract from Margaret Atwood's *The Handmaid's Tale*.

Text 2B

I open the front gate and close it behind me, looking down but not back. The sidewalk is red brick.

Extract from *The Handmaid's Tale*, Margaret Atwood,
Jonathan Cape (1985)

The Handmaid's Tale is narrated by a character, Offred, rather than by the author Margaret Atwood and it would be unconvincing for a reader to claim otherwise. In this case, it would be difficult to argue that the author and narrator are the same entity. It is, however, clear that Offred is an authorial construct and that Atwood uses Offred's fictional voice for a distinctive purpose. Readers are therefore very likely to attach some degree of intentionality to the use of a particular narrative perspective and assume that the use of a narrator, or narrators, is part of the overall design an author has in mind.

KEY TERM

Intentionality: the belief that an author has a reason for shaping a narrative in a particular way

---

Readers, and particularly students of literature, frequently refer to this idea of intentionality. For example, Text 2C is part of a post to goodreads, an online book reading community, on *The Handmaid's Tale*. In this post the contributor refers to Margaret Atwood and frames her comments in a way that shows her understanding of the relationship between author and narrator.

Text 2C

[…] Atwood describes life in the not too distant future where the United States has been transformed through military coup into a totalitarian theocracy. This dystopian horror story is made all the more real by the bridge Atwood has created between the world we know now and the world that could be […]

Extract from post to goodreads

Making a clear distinction between an author and a narrator but maintaining that there is a relationship between the two, means that it is possible to identify different levels of telling within a narrative. In reading and responding to *The Handmaid's Tale* for example it is useful to distinguish between a number of separate but related entities. First, there is the real-life Margaret Atwood. Most readers of her fiction won't actually know her and any information they do have will have been gained from reading biographies and book reviews and from listening to her being interviewed. These can only ever offer a partial and selective 'version' of her. For most readers therefore, the real author Margaret Atwood is largely inaccessible.

In contrast, a reader may feel that they have a clear sense of the person responsible for specifically writing *The Handmaid's Tale*, again relying on reading and reviews, this time exclusively about the novel. For example, Atwood has given interviews where she discusses the book and there is a significant body of reviews from both academic and non-academic readers. This version of Atwood is the implied author that readers might have in their minds when they read or talk about *The Handmaid's Tale*. Since this is a construct that is particular to this novel, a reader will construct a different implied author for

Atwood's first novel *The Edible Woman* (1969) or, at the time of writing, her last book, *Hag-Seed* (2016). In these cases, readers form a different impression and construct a different version of the author behind the work. In fact this way of thinking and talking about authors is commonplace. For example, critics and readers often talk about 'early Shakespeare' or 'late Shakespeare' plays. In doing so, the implied author they have in mind varies considerably: the Shakespeare behind *Titus Andronicus* is a newcomer to the Elizabethan theatre while the Shakespeare of *The Tempest* is a seasoned dramatist.

KEY TERMS

Real author: the real-life human entity responsible for writing a piece of fiction

Implied author: the conceptual entity that a reader creates and has in mind when they read a particular piece of fiction

In the case of *The Handmaid's Tale*, Offred is the narrator. Atwood may therefore permit Offred to speak in ways and voice opinions that are very different to her own to create certain effects. Overall, the relationship between these levels of telling is shown in Figure 2.1.

Figure 2.1: Levels of telling

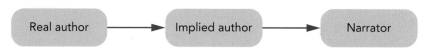

In some cases, readers may pick up on the apparent mismatch between the words of a narrator and what they perceive the implied author believes. This can result in a form of irony. For example, in Gillian Flynn's novel *Gone Girl* (2012) the two narrators, Nick and Amy, are revealed to be responsible for a number of criminal and unethical actions, presenting ideas and values that are clearly at odds with those of the author.

ACTIVITY 2.1

Exploring levels of telling

Explore the relationship and the tension between the roles of real author, implied author and narrator by thinking about a novel or poem that you know well and where you feel that there is a mismatch between what the narrator is saying and the stance of the implied author. Can you explain what this mismatch is and what effects you think it creates?

2

2.1.2 Irony and unreliability

As suggested above, a tension between different levels of telling may result in particular and interesting interpretative effects. For example, *The Handmaid's Tale* ends with a final chapter, 'Historical Notes', which consists of a transcript from a conference that takes place around two hundred years after the events in the novel. The main speaker, Professor James Darcy Pieixoto highlights how he had worked on reconstructing Offred's narrative from a series of recordings that had been discovered. Pieixoto reveals that he was largely responsible for organising the events into a narrative form and raises doubts about Offred's identity and her story. This may result in readers retrospectively speculating about the reliability of Offred's narrative. It may also seem ironic that the narrative that readers had been following is revealed to be something different to what they previously thought it was. Equally, Pieixoto demonstrates views that seem at odds with the overall message of the novel and certainly with what readers might assume to be the message of the implied author, Margaret Atwood. Ironically, his final words to his audience as he finishes his speech, 'Are there any questions?', can be viewed as an invitation to readers to question the accuracy of all that they have just read and assess their position towards the framing narrative that Pieixoto has provided.

Such examples of irony may lead readers to question the reliability of a speech, an extract or even a whole novel as they think about the extent to which a narrator's version of events is representative of the actual events they are reporting on. In some cases, a narrative will have an unreliable narrator and the reader will become aware that the narrator's account is not to be trusted.

The narratologist Greta Olsen (2003) explores unreliability in more detail by offering a useful distinction between what she terms a fallible narrator and an untrustworthy narrator. A fallible narrator is one who is mistaken about what they believe or who has limited knowledge of the events they are narrating. They may have only partial knowledge that means that they cannot provide a reliable version of events. In turn, their understanding of an event may be compromised by their age or by some mental deficiency. A fallible narrator is therefore usually affected by some external factor beyond their control.

KEY TERMS

Unreliable narrator: a narrator whose shaping of events is a distortion of actual events

Fallible narrator: a narrator whose unreliability is a result of partial or limited knowledge

Untrustworthy narrator: a narrator whose unreliability is a result of some internal characteristic or strong emotional involvement that causes them to distort the truth

In contrast, an untrustworthy narrator's unreliability is a result of more personal behaviours or traits. Olsen argues that this may be as a result of some deeply ingrained characteristic such as greed, anger or selfishness that motivates their decisions about how to report on and frame events. Equally, an untrustworthy narrator may have such a strong emotional involvement in their story that the subjectivity of their narrative naturally distorts the truth. Alternatively, an untrustworthy narrator may simply be a pathological liar!

Generally an unreliable narrator will display one or more of these specific characteristics:

- A tendency to contradict their own comments throughout their narrative

- Discrepancies between what they say and what they do

- Describe themselves in a way that clearly clashes with the views of other characters

- Make extended attempts to engage the reader's sympathy

- Provide admissions of memory loss, limited knowledge or prejudice.

ACTIVITY 2.2
Unreliability

Read Text 2D, an extract from *The Girl on the Train* by Paula Hawkins, a novel which has three unreliable narrators. In this extract, one of the narrators, Rachel, is recounting a visit to the police station where she gives an account of an incident to two officers: Riley and Gaskill. What aspects of Rachel's narrative mark her as potentially unreliable? Can you specify the particular linguistic markers that are evidence of this?

Text 2D

'I remembered the man,' I said. 'I told you there was a man at the station. I can describe him.' Riley raised her eyebrows ever so slightly and shifted in her seat. 'He was about medium height, medium build, reddish hair. I slipped on the steps and he caught my arm.' Gaskill leaned forward, his elbows on the table, hands clasped together in front of his mouth. 'He was wearing… I think he was wearing a blue shirt.'

This is not actually true. I do remember a man, and I'm pretty sure he had reddish hair, and I think that he smiled at me, or smirked at me, when I was on the train. I think that he got off at Witney, and I think he might have spoken to me. It's possible I might have slipped on the steps. I have a memory of it, but I can't tell whether the memory belongs to Saturday night or to another time. There have been many slips, on many staircases. I have no idea what he was wearing.

Extract from *The Girl on the Train*, Paula Hawkins, Black Swan (2015)

2.2 Point of view

Of course, any instance of narration can only offer a single perspective on an event. The incident described by Alan Sugar in Text 2A could be told from a number of alternative perspectives: from his mother, from someone working in Woolworths, a fellow shopper, the bus driver, and so on. Each perspective or point of view would offer a different take on what had happened.

KEY TERM

Point of view: the perspective from which the narrative unfolds

---

2.2.1 Telling and perceiving

You can start to explore point of view by distinguishing between *who tells* and *who perceives* a narrative. This is an important distinction that allows us to differentiate between two basic types of narration. On the one hand, homodiegetic narratives, where the narrator is internal to and participates in the story, are told from a first-person perspective and consequently use the first-person pronouns 'I' and 'we'. On the other hand heterodiegetic narratives, where the narrating voice is external to and does not participate in the story, are told in the third-person and make use of the third person pronouns 'he', 'she' and 'they'.

KEY TERM

Homodiegetic narrative: a first-person narrative where the narrator is usually also a character in the story-world

---

Homodiegetic narration is relatively straightforward to analyse since the character telling the story also perceives the events in that story. Both Text 2C and Text 2D are good examples of this type: the first-person perspective tells readers that the perception of events is from their particular and unique point of view.

In contrast, there are two possible forms of heterodiegetic narration. In the first, external heterodiegetic narration, the narrator speaks from a detached position and does not enter the consciousness of a specific character. In the second, the narrator may be narrating the events but not actually perceiving them. This is a kind of narrative 'trick', known as internal heterodiegetic narration, where the narrator moves into the mind of a character and filters events through that character's consciousness to show what they are thinking or feeling. Examples of these two narration types are shown in Text 2E from the opening to Charles Dickens' *Dombey and Son* (external) and in Text 2F from Jon McGregor's short story 'The singing' (internal).

KEY TERMS

External heterodiegetic narrative: a third-person narrative where the narrator is outside of the events of the story-world

Internal heterodiegetic narrative: a third-person account where the narrator filters their account through the consciousness of a particular character

---

Text 2E

Dombey sat in the corner of the darkened room in the great arm-chair by the bedside, and Son lay tucked up warm in a little basket bedstead, carefully disposed on a low settee immediately in front of the fire and close to it, as if his constitution were analogous to that of a muffin, and it was essential to toast him brown while he was very new.

Extract from *Dombey and Son*, Charles Dickens (1846–1848)

Text 2F

She lay very still, trying not to let the sound of the singing slip away. It was so vivid, yet so distant. This kept happening. She could never make out the words, if there were any, nor even quite a tune. She wasn't sure, really, whether it could properly be called singing.

Extract from 'The singing', Jon McGregor, Bloomsbury (2012)

A useful analogy to help remember these types is to imagine a film camera. In external narration, the camera operator simply films a scene from a detached position; in internal narration, the effect is more like a point of view shot. Of course in both of these types of narration, the camera will focus on different things. For example, imagine a narrative centred on the scene depicted in Figure 2.2.

Figure 2.2: Girl by the river

An external heterodiegetic narrative might be something like this:

> Sarah stands alone. Opposite her are buildings touching the grey sky. A single boat drifts along the river, passengers talking to each other in the cold air.

In this example, the detached view gives a sense of the entire picture; in this instance, a rather general overview of the scene is offered. The narrative is clearly from the perspective of the narrating voice rather than from any character in the scene.

In contrast an internal heterodiegetic narration, filtered through the consciousness of the main character, might be something like this:

> Sarah looks across the river, wondering who might be on the other side. She feels the cold air against her face, and is glad that she decided to wear a hat. Resting her right hand on the metal fence, she looks down towards the water.

In this example, the narrator allows access to Sarah's consciousness and the focus is on aspects of the scene that are more personal to her. Verbs such as 'looks', 'wondering', 'feels' and 'decided' position her rather than the narrator as the perceiver of the events. Equally, references to experiences that are felt by Sarah, 'cold air against her face, 'resting her right hand', anchor this narrative firmly within her experience. Even the adverb 'down' orientates the narrative from Sarah's perspective.

2.2.2 Space and time

A second aspect of point of view is that it may be framed in relation to space and time. As an example, re-read Alan Sugar's narrative (Text 2A). Here the narrative events are situated in a distinctive location via the use of prepositional phrases ('outside shops', 'from Stoke Newington') and spatial adverbs/adverb phrases ('inside', 'halfway home'). The events are also positioned in time through a prepositional phrase that introduces an overall time frame ('In the late forties'), a noun phrase ('One day') that begins the story when Sugar is lost, an adverb phrase ('back then') and the use of the past tense (e.g. 'went to', 'parked'), which situates the events in a different time zone to the time of telling.

In the original narrative, the events surrounding Sugar's mother forgetting him are sequenced and retold in chronological order. However, it would be possible to alter the perspective by introducing any number of flashbacks or flashforwards so as to reposition the time and/or place of telling. Imagine for example that the events were narrated as follows:

> One day, my mum went to Woolworths and parked me outside in my pram. Looking back at that time now, she realises how foolish she was to forget me. In her later years she often spoke about this incident and we all had a good laugh about it. I'm sure it was dangerous though. In fact she used to say that it reminded her of a time when she was younger and she had left a toy doll on a bus by mistake. She often did things like that as a child.

In this rewritten version, the time frame shifts forwards to a later time in which the mother is thinking back to the event and in which the narrator tells us that his family used to laugh about what had happened. Additionally, a further shift back to when the mother was younger reconfigures the narrative again so that the event detailed to us, losing a doll as a young girl, is now understood within the context of the mother being a much younger individual. In each case the shift in time anchors the narrative so that the story is understood from within a particular set of parameters.

2.2.3 Mind style

Finally, point of view may be related to an individual's way of seeing the world or thinking about events framed by a particular set of beliefs. This may be the result of a particular set of ideologies that a character or narrator has that results in them narrating in a certain way. More generally, the cognitive characteristics of a narrator are captured in the term mind style, first coined by the linguist Roger Fowler (1977) to explain how the way a character or narrator thinks and talks represents their mind. Fowler argued that evidence of a character's mind style might include details of the topics they talk about, the way they are ordered and the values they hold dear, all of which were realised through a range of linguistic expressions. Generally, aspects of mind style might be demonstrated through words and phrases that present a personal perspective on events, for example modal verbs, adjectives and adverbs to stress belief or commitment, verbs of perception and the use of words and phrases from a character's personal vocabulary.

KEY TERM

Mind style: the distinctive way that a character's/narrator's mental self is shown through the language that they use

---

An interesting way to explore mind style is to look at a narrative in which the narrator thinks or behaves in an unconventional way. For example, read Text 2G, an extract from Emily Barr's young adult novel *The One Memory of Flora Banks*. The main protagonist and narrator, Flora, is 17 years old but suffers from anterograde amnesia, which means that she cannot remember anything past her tenth birthday. Flora writes messages on her arm to remind herself of her age and to keep her safe but her amnesia significantly colours her narration. In this extract she has just left a party at night and is walking on her own.

Text 2G

> I am standing in the middle of the road, and it is night. I look around, trying to work it out. There is a white line under my feet. This is the exact middle of the road. A car comes towards me, fast, and honks its horn. I stare at the headlights as they come closer, but it swerves and carries on going, its horn still sounding as it vanishes into the distance.
>
> I should not be out on my own. I shouldn't stand in the middle of roads. I have only just been allowed to start crossing roads without a grown-up. Why am I out in the dark? Why am I alone? Where is my mum?

Extract form *The One Memory of Flora Banks*,
Emily Barr, Penguin (2017)

There are several aspects of this narrative which reveal Flora's mind style. Content-wise, her narrative is focused on the elementary and child-like emotion of being lost. She makes reference to being unaware of where she is and what she needs to do, refers to the fact that she shouldn't be out on her own, and looks around for her mother. She is clearly thinking like a ten-year old rather than a seventeen-year old.

Flora also presents these thoughts in a child-like way. She uses single-clause or double-clause sentences, which have very straightforward structures and are relatively short in length. Nearly all of these sentences begin with 'I' or have some other very simple subject and, in the second paragraph, the final three sentences are framed as questions. These questions represent a mind that is desperately trying to work out where she is and what she needs to do next as her fear and anxiety grow. Equally, the simple lexis ('white line', 'grown-up', and 'mum') are words more associated with a child with limited knowledge of her situation than with a mature teenager. Taken together, these linguistic markers all help the reader to understand Flora's mind in the midst of the panic of memory loss.

2.3 Modal grammar

One specific way that a narrator can demonstrate their point of view is through the use of modal expressions. This section briefly introduces Paul Simpson's (1993) modal grammar, a framework that allows for more intricate analysis of a particular narrative style.

In linguistics, modality is the umbrella term used to describe language that presents an individual's opinion of, or commitment to, any state of affairs. Modality may be shown through a number of different word classes and types of expression. One of the most common ways that modality is expressed is through the use of modal auxiliary verbs such as 'may', 'might', 'would', 'should' and 'must'. These generally combine with main verbs to emphasise varying degrees of certainty or necessity. In other cases, however, modality can also be realised in these linguistic forms:

- modal lexical verbs, e.g. 'like', 'hope', 'believe'

- modal adjectives, e.g. 'sure', 'certain', 'doubtful'

- modal adverbs, e.g. 'perhaps', 'possibly', 'maybe'

- modal tags, e.g. 'I guess'.

It is possible to classify modality depending on the type of commitment that a word or expression emphasises. Broadly speaking, each of the following categories highlight a different sense of meaning.

Deontic modality: expressions that highlight a sense of obligation or necessity

'You <u>must</u> come back' (modal auxiliary verb)

'It is <u>necessary</u> for you to come back' (modal adjective)

KEY TERMS

Modality: the term used to describe language that presents degrees of attitude or commitment

Deontic modality: expressions that highlight a sense of obligation or necessity

---

Narrative

Boulomaic modality: expressions that highlight aspects of desire

'I hope you will come back' (modal lexical verb)

'Hopefully, you will come back' (modal adverb)

Epistemic modality: expressions that highlight degrees of belief, certainty or perception

'You might come back' (modal auxiliary verb)

'I think you'll come back' (modal lexical verb)

'You'll come back, I guess' (modal tag)

'It's clear that you are coming back' (modal adjective)

It's worth remembering that these categories are broad and that some modal auxiliary verbs can behave in different ways depending on how they are used. For example, 'must' can have both a deontic and an epistemic sense as demonstrated below.

- You must leave now (deontic sense showing necessity)

- This must be the one we are looking for (epistemic sense showing a degree of certainty)

Simpson's modal grammar uses this way of conceptualising modality by incorporating it into the model of narration types that you explored in section 2.2.1. Simpson differentiates between homodiegetic and heterodiegetic narration, and between heterodiegetic narration where the narrator is detached (he calls this the narratorial mode) and where the narrative is filtered through the consciousness of a character (he calls this the reflector mode). Simpson also argues that narratives may be classified by what he terms their dominant modal shading:

- **Positively shaded narrative:** the prominent use of deontic and boulomaic forms, and/or epistemic forms that show strong certainty together with evaluative adjectives and adverbs.

- **Negatively shaded narrative:** the prominent use of epistemic forms that display uncertainty and/or anxiety.

- **Neutrally shaded narrative:** a flat narrative with little or no modalised expressions.

KEY TERMS

Boulomaic modality: expressions that highlight aspects of desire

Epistemic modality: expressions that highlight degrees of belief, certainty or perception

Modal shading: the dominant type of modality in a text

ACTIVITY 2.3

Rewriting modal shading

A useful way of exploring the effects of modal shading is to take a short extract that has one dominant pattern and rewrite it into the other two modes. For example, Text 2H is the opening to 'I could see the smallest things, a short story by Raymond Carver, and would, in Simpson's model, be a neutrally shaded narrative. Can you replace this into positively shaded and negatively shaded versions? Which words and phrases have you changed and what do you notice about the overall 'feel' of your two new texts?

Text 2H

I was in bed when I heard the gate. I listened carefully: I didn't hear anything else. But I heard that. I tried to wake Cliff. He was passed out. So I got up and went to the window. A big moon was laid over the mountains that went around the city. It was a white moon and covered with scars.

Extract from *I could see the smallest things*,
Raymond Carver, Vintage (1981)

2.4 Multimodal narratives

In this final section, you will explore a particular type of written narrative. A multimodal narrative is one that combines different communicative modes such as words, images, sounds, gesture and space. A multimodal analysis will therefore move beyond examining words alone, and instead explore how those words link with other resources that narrators can draw on in order to make meaning. Although in the forthcoming sections you will focus specifically on narratives that combine words with images, you could explore multimodality in more detail by looking back at some of the texts you have already read both in this chapter and in Chapter 1 to consider the extent to which they draw on different modes. In effect, almost every narrative you come across will rely on some combination of different modes to tell its story.

KEY TERM

Multimodal narrative: a narrative that draws on and combines different communicative modes

---

2.4.1 Advertisements

Advertising is a genre that treats narrative in a particular way. Since the purposes of an advertisement are to inform someone of a product or service and persuade them to buy it, the genre works by presenting a contrast between the actual world and what that world could (and would) be like were the consumer to buy the product being offered. In other words, advertising invites the reader/ potential buyer to construct a narrative by projecting something that is extremely attractive and desirable.

As an example of this, look at Text 2I, an advertisement for a stove manufacturer in the UK.

Text 2I

As discussed in Chapter 1, it is almost impossible to look at an image and not understand it within the parameters of some narrative frame. In this instance, the image tells a story in its own right: the sofa in the background has been deserted in favour of a position in front of the stove, complete with cushions, a drink and a snack. Of course, these entities also assume the presence of an individual (or individuals); the reader's built-in narrative device will probably lend itself to imagining a situation where someone has left the sofa for the warmer and more comfortable place next to the stove. The advertisement thus projects a narrative of desire and need and asks that the reader imagine a future where, having bought the stove, they are sitting in front of it! Indeed, the desire to encourage readers to imagine themselves as the ideal reader of this advertisement may be why the company has chosen not to show an actual person sitting in front of the stove.

Of course, the image in this advertisement works in conjunction with the words 'Nothing warms better'. These words form a structure in their own right and separately project a message by claiming the exceptional, unrivalled nature of the product, and playing on the dual sense of the verb 'warms' as both causing a rise in temperature and producing positive feelings. However, the words also clearly support the image, both in the message that they send about the product and, noticeably, in the fact that 'warms' is in orange to match the glow of the flames in the stove. In fact, advertisements often make use of and connect these complementary modes in this way. This is often termed text–image cohesion. Although each of these modes could be analysed separately, together they provide a more powerful message about the product being advertised.

Advertisements may also draw on multimodal aspects of point of view to help convey their message. For example in Text 2J, an advertisement for an upmarket men's clothing company, the model is looking downwards with the implication that he is at a higher level than the reader. The linguists Gunther Kress and Theo van Leeuwen (1996) argue that models in advertisements are often positioned to look down on the reader and consequently position the advertiser in a position of power. A useful analogy here is that of the low angle shot: the subject is photographed from below eye level and so appears larger and more powerful. In contrast, Kress and van Leeuwen suggest that products in advertisements are often presented so as to suggest that the reader is looking down on them. In a high angle photographic shot, a subject will appear lower than the reader and consequently less powerful; Kress and van Leeuwen argue that this narrative trick is used in advertising to make products appear within reach of the reader and consequently more appealing. An example of this is shown in Text 2K, an advertisement for a food company.

KEY TERMS

Ideal reader: the reader who agrees with the world-view projected in a text

Text–image cohesion: the way that text and images work together to create a sense of meaning

Text 2J

Text 2K

Text 2L

Masterpiece of Intelligence.

Mercedes-Benz

PRACTICE QUESTION
Analysing an advertisement

Look at Text 2L, an advertisement for Mercedes-Benz. Analyse this advertisement in terms of the lifestyle it projects, text–image cohesion and narrative point of view.

2.4.2 Graphic narratives

Another type of text that plays with storytelling in an interesting way is the graphic narrative. Graphic narratives may include adaptations of text-only novels (usually termed graphic novels), comic books and publishing sub-genres such as Japanese manga. Compared to conventional text-only novels, graphic narratives draw on the same kinds of strategies as advertising, for example text-image cohesion and the use of space and visual angles to suggest point of view.

According to the narratologist Pascal Lefèvre, graphic narratives offer a very distinctive reading experience since '[…] the medium itself offers multiple possibilities for storytelling, even as it imposes limitations on how the story can be told.' (2011: 31). As an illustration of this, look at Text 2M, six panels from the the graphic novel *Breaks* by Emma Vieceli and Malin Ryden.

Text 2M

Extract from 'BREAKS', Emma Vieceli and Malin Ryden
(Soaring Penguin Press, 2017)

One central idea behind graphic narratives is that time is handled in a very different way. In prose fiction, an author is able to set out the temporal parameters through the use of tense and through specifying the duration of events. However, as you can see in Text 2I, this is not possible in graphic narratives. In fact, one of the limitations of the medium is that the reader has to decide on how much time has passed between the events shown in each of the panels. For example in panel 3, the two characters are talking and the reader is left to decide how long passes between that panel and panel 4 (the telephone ringing and Tanner picking it up) as well as the duration leading to panel 5 (the call ending and Tanner and the female character speaking to each other again). In a similar way, the reader will need to make connections between each of these panels to establish a sense of a story. In Text 2M, some of these connections (for example between panel 2 and panel 3) are obvious but on other occasions the reader is required to infer what might be happening to 'fill in' narrative gaps in order to make sense of the narrative and to construct some coherent frame of reference from which the rest of the story can be understood. This might involve establishing the emotions of the female character in panel 5, for example is she angry or anxious? And, what is she thinking as she touches Tanner on the arm in panel 6? You can explore the extent to which graphic narratives demand this of their readers by thinking of all the possible events, situations, emotions and feelings that each of the panels – and the panels combined – might suggest.

RESEARCH QUESTION
Graphic narratives

An interesting exercise to explore the ways that graphic narratives operate would be to compare an extract from a purely written narrative with its graphic novel adaptation. What do you notice about the way that the two present the same narrative material? How is narrative time handled in the graphic novel version? How are images used to replace the words of the source text? There are plenty of pairs of texts that you might choose. Some suggestions are offered below; the original text's author and publisher is given first, followed by those of the author/illustrator of the graphic novel.

- *City of Glass* (Paul Auster, Faber and Faber; Paul Karasik and David Mazzucchelli, Picador)

- *Fahrenheit 451* (Ray Bradbury, Flamingo; Tim Hamilton, Hill and Wang)

- *The Graveyard Book* (Neil Gaiman, Bloomsbury; P. Craig Russell, HarperCollins)

- *The Lottery* (Shirley Jackson, Viking Press; Miles Hyman, Hill and Wang)

In addition, Classical Comics produce graphic novel versions (generally for a younger audience) of established English literary classics. You can find details of their publications at www.cambridge.org/links/escnar6002

Wider reading

You can find out more about the topics in this chapter by reading the following:

Authors and narrators

Leech, G. and Short, M. (2007) *Style in Fiction: A Linguistic Introduction to English Fictional Prose* (Second edition). Harlow: Longman.

Point of view

Toolan, M. (2001) *Narrative: A Critical Linguistic Introduction* (Second edition). London: Routledge.

Modal grammar

Simpson, P. (1993) *Language, Ideology and Point of View*. London: Routledge.

Multimodal narratives

Cohn, N. (2016) *The Visual Narrative Reader*. London: Bloomsbury.

Kress, G. and van Leeuwen, T. (1996) *Reading Images: The Grammar of Visual Design*. Oxon: Routledge.

Saraceni, M. (2003) *The Language of Comics*. London: Routledge.

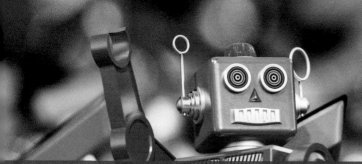

Chapter 3
Spoken narratives

In this chapter you will:

- Understand and explore different ways of describing and analysing spoken narratives

- Develop your understanding of tellability

- Examine how narrators frame their experiences of places in narratives

3.1 'Big' and 'small' stories: narrative and identity

In this section, you will examine two particular kinds of story. In the first, you will look at an established model for analysing one-speaker narratives, drawing on research carried out by the narratologist William Labov. In this instance, the focus will be on how speakers form fully rounded narratives and how these might be explained in terms of their structure. In the second, you'll look at stories that are shorter and less defined, largely focusing on how speakers tell these as part of a larger practice of maintaining social connections in a group.

In both of these cases, you will draw on an important idea in the study of narrative and in linguistics more generally: that speakers construct identities as they use language and that the identities they wish to construct depend on the situations that they find themselves in.

The idea of identity as a construction is an important one and runs against a more traditional view that speakers talk as they do simply because of who they are and where they come from. In contrast, an emphasis on construction gives more emphasis on the linguistic decisions individuals make as they choose to project an identity for themselves through the way they speak. In other words, they *perform* an identity that they want other speakers and hearers to understand. A useful analogy would be to imagine language as a resource like the clothes that we wear, the books we read or the music we listen to: we use all of these to project an impression that we want others to see. Often, of course, such choices come together in 'About me' sections of social media pages or personal websites where individuals present narratives of themselves together with photographs, details of their interests, and so on.

The linguist Harvey Sacks (1984) argued that this performativity was an essential part of how speakers presented themselves as ordinary – and therefore trustworthy – through the everyday stories they told to their friends and relatives. Sacks argued that in much conversation, people talk about 'ordinary' things such as the time of day and the weather, what was on television the previous evening and how they feel (well, sick, and so on). Underpinning these conversations is a sense that speakers are performing a role in light of what is expected of them: Sacks argues that not talking about these topics in everyday conversation would mark an individual out as different in some way. Put simply, we expect people to talk about these sorts of things!

3.1.1 The structure of oral narratives

One of the most famous and widely used models for examining one-speaker narratives was developed by William Labov (1972). Labov drew on his extensive fieldwork on New York Black English vernacular to put together his model.

Labov had asked participants to tell him personal stories that he then recorded and analysed in terms of their structure. From his data, he concluded that the narratives tended to follow a fairly common pattern that involved the following elements or stages:

- **Abstract (A):** an indication that the speaker wants a listener's attention and is signalling the start of the narrative.

- **Orientation (O):** the 'who', 'where', 'what' and 'why'. This sets the scene and provides background information that the speaker sees as important.

- **Complicating action (CA):** the main body of the narrative.

- **Evaluation (E):** the speaker stepping outside of the narrative to explain why the story is interesting.

- **Resolution (R):** the ending of the narrative that ties up loose ends and provides closure.

- **Coda (C):** a signal that the narrative has ended.

In order to see how this structure might be applied to a spoken narrative, read Text 3A. This is part of a series of stories narrated by a middle-aged female speaker to a friend.

Text 3A

This is what happened, yesterday I was sitting listening to the radio when the lights suddenly went off. It was suddenly pitch black and I couldn't see anything. This is the funny part though, a programme came on the radio about the war and how in air raids everything was dark. I really understood what it must have been like! I had to find my candles and light a couple. After a while though the lights came back on. Must have been a short power cut. Isn't that odd?

Key

Abstract

Orientation

Complicating action

Evaluation

Resolution

Coda

Narrative

A particularly interesting element of Labov's model is the evaluation. Labov argued that the purpose of an evaluation was to emphasis a story's tellability (see Chapter 1). Labov suggested that whilst evaluations could typically occur at any point in a story, they tended to appear at the beginning in order to emphasise that a story would be worth telling or else just before any climactic events (close to the transition between complicating action and resolution) in order for the speaker to increase tension and maintain their listener's attention. Indeed this can be seen in Text 3A where the speaker's second evaluation 'I really understood what it must have been like!' acts as a delaying tactic that increases anticipation as her listener waits for the climax of the story. Consequently, evaluative comment is often used by speakers to make their stories appear more personal and more attractive: the subjectivity of evaluation means that attention is taken away from the story itself and back to the speaker's own involvement in or relationship to the events.

Labov also suggested that there were two different types of evaluation. In the first, external evaluation, the narrator breaks from the main narrative to offer their perspective on the story. This is the type of evaluation offered by the speaker in Text 3A where an evaluation is added at the time of recounting; the original words were not part of the narrative events. In contrast, internal evaluation is arguably more subtle and complex. Here a narrator makes comments that are within the same time frame as the main narrative and are interwoven into the events of the story.

KEY TERMS

External evaluation: an expression of attitude towards the events where the speaker 'stands back' from the main action

Internal evaluation: an expression of attitude towards the events in a narrative that occur in the same time frame as the main action

Labov suggested that there were four subtypes of internal evaluation:

- **Intensifiers** that strengthen the force of a particular word or phrase. This could be in the form of a gesture, the use of repetition (e.g. 'that bad bad child') or an onomatopoeic word (e.g 'I heard this massive BANG!')

- **Comparators** that draw attention to what didn't happen either through negation (e.g. 'You have never seen such an event'), or reference to future or hypothetical events (e.g. 'I'll be more careful next time').

- **Correlatives** that bring events together into a single event so that one acts to evaluate the other. This is often through the use of participles to suspend the narrative and provide suspense (e.g. 'We were sitting at the station, waiting, just sitting there, talking to each other'), nouns/noun phrases in apposition that provide more detail (e.g. 'He drove a car, a large red car'), or so-called left-hand participle) (e.g. 'a shifty-looking character in the car').

- **Explicatives** that qualify and give reasons for particular narrative events and are introduced by clauses beginning with *while, though, since* or *because* (e.g. 'I had to leave because I was so tired').

Labov's narrative categories can be summarised in Figure 3.1, which is based on Labov's own diagrammatic representation of his work (Labov 1972: 369). The various types of evaluation discussed above may occur at any point during the narrative and are therefore placed in the middle.

Figure 3.1: Labov's internal structure of a narrative

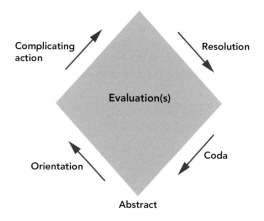

ACTIVITY 3.1
Exploring Labov's narrative structure

A good way to explore the usefulness of Labov's model is to record and transcribe some narratives yourself. You could replicate Labov's approach by asking friends or family members to talk about an event or personal experience they remember. Once you have transcribed your data, code the narrative using Labov's elements, paying careful attention to transition points (e.g. where complicating action becomes resolution) and the different types of evaluation that speakers use. If you can collect data from several people you could compare their use of evaluative strategies.

As you generate your data, do bear in mind ethics (let people know they are being recorded), the observer's paradox (the idea that people may talk differently if they know they are being observed and recorded) and the fact that speakers will have varying degrees of narrative competence that impact on their ability to tell a story. For example, very young children may not produce as complex narratives as adults.

3.1.2 Small stories

Labov's model provides a way of examining and analysing extended narratives but often, of course, the stories we tell aren't always fully formed or structured in the same way as Text 3A. In many cases, narratives are fleeting, unfinished, hypothetical or ongoing in that speakers will narrate parts and return to them later to complete. Narratives like these are sometimes known as small stories. Small stories do by their nature tend to be short, but more importantly their defining feature is that they generally function to establish and maintain some kind of social connection between a speaker and a group of listeners. Small stories are usually embedded in a local context where participants draw on extensive shared background knowledge as they speak. This is usually a clearly defined social space known as a site of engagement (Scollon 1998) that allows groups of people to come together to engage in a particular form of social practice, for example in a friendship group or in a service encounter.

KEY TERM

Site of engagement: a social space in which groups of people come together to engage in a particular type of social practice

---

Small stories are therefore largely the stories that people tell in everyday settings and are often concerned with everyday matters and events. They also tend to be concerned with immediacy; speakers generally talk about very recent past or near future events, and often stories are introduced and then dropped very quickly without any real development. For example, look at Text 3B, part of a conversation between two friends.

Text 3B

A: What are we doing today?

B: Wait isn't the game on television later?

A: No it's in the evening

B: Yeah but do you remember when the quarter-final was played at six and they put it on live?

A: Oh yeah. And Dave came round to watch

B: Let's check the time then

In this text, the friends are discussing the time of a football match later that evening, but introduce two fleeting stories relevant to their discussion. First, the previous time that a game starting at six o'clock was televised and second, the additional fact that another friend called Dave joined them in watching it. Neither of these stories is expanded and both speakers are happy for the stories to remain fleeting as they move on to make their plans for later.

The sociolinguist Alexandra Georgakopoulou (2007) has conducted research into small stories and how they get used by groups. Georgakopoulou argues that speakers often present what she calls 'breaking news' in the form of a short story, which can be effortlessly dropped into conversation, emphasising that they are dynamic narratives that speakers draw on for quick and maximum impact. Georgakopoulou's research also demonstrates that small stories are often a feature of exchanges on social media, email and text messages, all of which tend to be used for shorter exchanges by participants. You can see an example of this in Text 3C, a full exchange via text message between two friends. In this instance, they were sharing and discussing the 'breaking news' that Claudio Ranieri, the football manager who had amazingly won the English Premier League with the unfancied Leicester City in 2016, had been sacked nine months later. The story is shared over the course of five short turns.

Text 3C

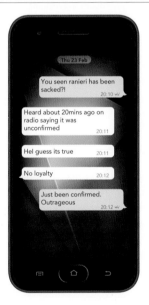

3.2 Co-constructing narratives

3.2.1 Interaction in talk

The discussion in the previous section identified how stories are often told within groups and how people interact as they perform narratives.

Narrative

Multi-speaker interaction, where speakers share conversational space and speaking time to create a successful conversation, can be analysed using the idea of a conversational turn. The simplest unit within the turn is the adjacency pair, two utterances that naturally combine and where the second pair part provides a response to the first pair part. An example of an adjacency pair is in Text 3D.

> ### KEY TERM
> **Adjacency pair:** a structure of two turns: a first pair part and second pair part

Text 3D

> A: Would you like a drink? (first pair part)
>
> B: Yes please (second pair part)

Text 3D is an example of a question–answer adjacency pair. Other types of adjacency pairs that occur commonly in spoken language include:

- summons–answer

- greeting–greeting

- goodbye–goodbye

- invitation–accept or decline

- request–grant or deny

In each case, there is an expectation that a speaker will produce an appropriate response. For example, saying 'hello' to a friend and not receiving a response back would be considered rude in most cultures and contexts. A first pair part therefore assumes that a relevant second pair part will follow. For those types of adjacency pairs that have two possible second pair parts, one will be more socially acceptable than the other. For example, look at Text 3E which contains a request–grant adjacency pair.

Text 3E

> A: Can I leave the room? (first pair part)
>
> B: Yes of course (second pair part)

In this case, a second pair part that grants the request is clearly more acceptable than one which denies it. If speaker B had said 'No', this would have been potentially embarrassing for both speakers and would clearly be viewed as a face-threatening act. In this instance, 'Yes of course' is a preferred response and 'No' is a dispreferred response. Of course, what is deemed preferred and dispreferred can vary from culture to culture.

In many instances of conversation, turns do not form neat pairs and conversation can move rapidly in a much looser way. Equally, speakers may insert other turns, known as an insertion sequence, between the two parts of an adjacency pair. Overall, the entire interaction between speakers is known as an exchange structure.

Within multi-speaker interaction, speakers will also tend to evaluate what each other has said, passing judgements and assessing the extent to which they agree or disagree with something. The linguist Anita Pomerantz (1984) refers to this kind of activity as assessment making. In a similar way to a straightforward adjacency pair, assessments largely invite either preferred or dispreferred responses. For example, when a speaker makes an assessment, the preferred response would be that a second speaker agrees with them. Pomerantz suggests that when there is some disagreement, a second speaker will attempt to reframe the initial assessment by making either an upgrade or a downgrade. In this way, a speaker can present a disagreement in a less confrontational way. These three types are shown in Text 3F.

KEY TERMS

Face-threatening act: a speech act that has the potential to damage someone's self-esteem

Preferred response: a second part of an adjacency pair that fits in with what the speaker of the first part expects to hear

Dispreferred response: a second part of an adjacency pair that doesn't fit in with what the speaker of the first part expects to hear

Insertion sequence: an additional sequence between the two parts of an adjacency pair

Exchange structure: sequence of turns between speakers

Assessment making: the act of evaluating something or someone when talking to others

Upgrade: the raising of the intensity of a speaker's assessment in a response to it

Downgrade: the lowering of the intensity of a speaker's assessment in a response to it

Text 3F

A: That's a beautiful coat (first pair part)

B: Yes it is (second pair part agreement)

A: That's a beautiful coat (first pair part)

B: Yes it's stunning (second pair upgrade)

A: That's a beautiful coat (first pair part)

B: Yes it's nice (second pair part downgrade)

3.2.2 Goodwin's model of storytelling

Charles Goodwin (1984) proposed a model that draws on ideas about interaction in talk and integrates them into theories of narrative and storytelling. Using a corpus of spoken data, Goodwin identified a series of interactional techniques that he saw were being used by speakers and listeners to help support them to tell their stories and position themselves as storytellers or to demonstrate that they wanted to hear the story and/or make a judgement on it. His seven techniques are listed below.

- **Story preface:** a signal that a speaker wants to tell a story and an invitation for others to show interest

- **Story solicit:** a response from someone else that they want to listen to the story

- **Preliminary to the story:** background information to the story in the form of the 'who', 'where', 'what' and 'why'

- **Story action:** the main body of the narrative

- **Parenthesis:** a strategy a speaker uses – in a similar way to Labov's term *evaluation* – to provide background detail that is outside of the narrative content itself. Its function is to support the story or to add richer descriptions of events and/or people

- **Story climax:** the conclusion of the narrative

- **Story appreciation:** signals from the audience that communicate their response to the narrative. This might be at several points during the story or at the end and could consist of questions, agreements and laughter or other emotions

Goodwin's model is a useful one as it is more firmly rooted in interaction than Labov's, and as such will allow you to analyse data in a way that takes account of both the narrator and the narratee's roles.

3.2.3 Narrative and gesture

Goodwin's research also involved exploring how narrators used gestures when they told their stories. In particular, he looked at how gestures were used to signpost particular elements or stages. For example, in an analysis of one speaker's narrative, he found that she supported her story preface by making a particular gesture and then used different gestures, together with other physical movements such as changing posture as she moved on to different parts of her story. Intriguingly, Goodwin's analysis revealed how the narrator's shift to a secondary narrative was accompanied by one specific gesture, which she then stopped using as she moved back into her main story.

Gesture is more generally a key tool that narrators use to help them tell their stories, and is an important part of communication itself. Indeed many linguists believe that gesture is a forerunner of speech; this can be seen in how gestures such as pointing are used by very young children as an early communicative tool before they learn to speak. David McNeill (2005) suggests that there are four main types of gesture that are used to support adult speech:

- **Iconic:** these resemble words that are spoken, for example describing driving a car and gesturing as though holding a steering wheel.

- **Metaphoric:** these represent a metaphorical idea being talked about by the speaker, for example a speaker describing feeling happy by raising their arms above their head. In this instance, the speaker is drawing on a common metaphor HAPPINESS IS UP: (this can be seen in verbal expressions such as 'I'm feeling high' and 'I'm on top of the world').

- **Deictic:** these are gestures that point towards something in the immediate vicinity or in a different location or time frame, for example a speaker mentioning something that happened the previous day and nodding their head backwards to 'point' towards that prior time (see also Chapter 4 on deixis).

- **Beat:** these are emphatic gestures that are used to signal important moments in narrative such as the arrival of a new character or an important plot development.

3.2.4 Tellability revisited

In Chapter 1, you explored the idea that stories may have high or low tellability. Indeed, in that chapter, tellability was defined as a key aspect of a story's content; in effect, the more tellable a story, the more likely that a listener would be interested and a speaker able to tell their tale. Given the focus of this chapter on interaction and the ways in which speakers and listeners come together to share experiences through narratives, it is worth revisiting tellability briefly to examine another way of thinking about this concept and its central position in storytelling.

Elinor Ochs and Lisa Capps (2001) argue that often tellability is not immediately obvious to participants when they engage in conversation. They suggest that a narrative that is seen to be tellable may well be one that is defined in relation to its *impact* rather than its *content*. In other words, it could be argued that a story is not inherently tellable but rather that it relies on its ability to make an emotional connection with its listener.

This view of tellability means that it is important to consider the context in which a story gets told. As Neal R. Norrick (2007: 135) argues:

> [...] tellability depends not only on the (detached) content of a narrative but also on the contextual (embedded) relevance of the story for the participants

involved [...] the tellability of familiar stories hinges not on their content as such but on the dynamics of the narrative event itself, and humor makes co-narration desirable.

In order to exemplify this idea, read Text 3G, a conversation between two friends talking about restaurants.

Text 3G

A: My folks were, um, we were visiting Los Angeles or something. And I remember being taken to a real fancy Mexican *restaurant* there, called Senor, something

   ((*laughter*))

B: Yeah.

A: Senor Pico, or something like,

   ((*laughter*))

A: And, you know, I hated everything.

B: Did you?

   ((*laughter*))

A: At the time I just hated

B: Mexican, yeah.

A: Mexican food. I'd, I'd love to go to some place like that now,

B: Yeah.

A: Where it's, you know, a real Mexican restaurant,

B: Yeah.

A: Because I like it.

B: Yeah. What kind of, what kind, do you like, uh, like Chinese or Italian or

A: I, um, I like Chinese and I should experiment more. The problem is, that my favorite food in the world is cashew chicken.

B: Oh, yeah.

A: So any time I go to a Chinese restaurant I want cashew chicken

   ((*laughter*))

Cambridge International Corpus

In this text, the content being discussed (the talk of different restaurants) is fairly mundane; the tellability of the story clearly rests in the fact that it is being told within a group with the two speakers developing the narrative together. The social aspect is apparent in the way that the speakers support each other and are at ease, evident in their laughter. This interaction demonstrates that the story's impact is fundamentally a social one; the tellability of the story can be claimed on the basis that it serves to maintain personal ties rather than being newsworthy in its own right.

3.3 Stories about place

3.3.1 Space and place

Narratives are often closely linked to specific locations that hold memories for a speaker. For example, think of a place that you remember from your childhood, perhaps somewhere that you used to visit regularly or where you had a memorable holiday. The chances are that you will remember it in narrative terms. It is no surprise then that many narratives involve speakers reflecting on the importance of a particular location to them. Indeed Mike Crang (1998) argues that people often define themselves through the places they have visited and the experiences they have had there. For Crang, the sense of place that is captured in a narrative is an essential part of who the narrator is.

Crang uses the term 'time-thickened' (1998: 103) to explain how a space (a location) becomes a place (a collection of memories). He argues that people's interactions with locations over time means that they invest emotions in them and gain a sense of belonging. A place, then, is something that people become attached to, and there is evidence of this in the stories that they tell. As an example, read Text 3H. In this text, the narrator is remembering and talking about her favourite place in Paris, an outdoor park that she used to visit as a child.

Text 3H

> There were some sort of old ruins that were scattered there. I'm not sure how legitimate they were. I think they were probably just placed there but they were fun to climb on and just be near or you could be near the waterfall, and listen to the sound of water rushing down, it made it a nice comfortable spot for hanging out with friends.

It is interesting that in this narrative, the speaker frames her initial story through the use of markers that show her stance towards the authenticity of her memories. These are largely markers of epistemic modality such as 'sort of', 'I'm not sure', 'I think' and 'probably', all of which demonstrate that she is initially unsure about some aspect of the place or her memories of it. However, the remainder of the narrative is framed in more certain terms. Here, she highlights the significance of the park to her and her sense of attachment by expressing her memories in terms that emphasise a closeness and physical attachment to specific parts of the park. For example, she uses the deictic adverb 'there' to set up a relationship between her and the park before using the prepositional phrase 'near the waterfall' and the noun phrases 'sound of water' and 'comfortable spot' to emphasise the physical aspects of her experience and show a perceived sense of closeness with the place she is describing.

KEY TERM

epistemic modality: expressions that highlight degrees of belief, certainty or perception

Narratives describing places often also draw attention to how a place has changed over time and relate that to a personal experience or attachment that a narrator has. Often this is shown through narratives that explicitly draw attention to some kind of physical connection between an individual and a place. For example, read Text 3I, an extract from the same narrative as Text 3H.

Text 3I

And it started off as just where I went to play. It was near a bilingual school my friends went to so we used to go and play in the park there and they had these ponies that you could get rides on and go all the way around the park, now, looking back I feel a bit sorry for them because they were probably not treated very well but it was nice back then to be able to sit on a pony and go riding.

In this text, the narrator uses the past tense forms 'started off' and 'used to go' as well as the adverbials 'looking back' and 'back then' to show her connection with the place she is describing. Equally, she makes extensive use of spatial terms such as the deictics (see Chapter 4) 'there', these', 'now' and the preposition 'around' to align herself with the location she is describing.

Finally, narrators often frame their narratives about places in very personal ways as they give their perspective on what they remember. For example, in Text 3J, again from the same narrative as Texts 3H and 3I, the narrator uses the verbs 'storming' and 'wandering' to describe the people she is describing. Interestingly, she also makes the story more tellable by imagining what the tourists are thinking and saying 'maybe we should take pictures of this, maybe it's relevant, is it very Parisian? I'm sure it's very chic, let's take a picture anyway, go stand there' as they walk around the park. Thus a relatively mundane event is remembered and retold as something much more attractive and framed in a way so as to make it interesting for the listener.

Text 3J

You could smell the cigarettes, and literally storming through the park to people who just sort of, just wandering through not entirely sure where they are, thinking, maybe we should take pictures of this, maybe it's relevant, is it very Parisian? I'm sure it's very chic, let's take a picture anyway, go stand there.

ACTIVITY 3.3
Narratives of place

Read Text 3K. The narrator is talking about a memory of a beach she used to visit. How does she talk about her experience and what strategies does she use to frame her narrative?

Text 3K

But to get down to the beach you had to walk down a real steep embankment. I mean, it was so steep they had put railroad ties as stair steps every once in a while, mainly for the erosion and that became a path as it were […] But the beach was beautiful. We managed to comb out some of the broken glass and the like, but the actual sand was a real good quality and real deep and we set up the old volleyball net and, you know, just a typical, uh, twenty or thirty guys playing volleyball on the beach and this, this cove, this beach was a bit of a cove and it was surrounded, oh, I'd say a couple of hundred yards by, uh, this hill, this mountainous, uh, rock terrain and only that little bitty section of it was actually beach. The rest of it was water right up against the rock.

Cambridge International Corpus

PRACTICE QUESTION
Analysing speakers and their experiences

Read Text 3L, a conversation between two friends discussing a visit to Italy. Analyse how they talk about their experiences. You could think about:

- how the speakers talk about themselves in relation to the places they have visited

- how they interact and co-construct their narrative

- the attitudes they present towards places and events.

Text 3L

A: I loved all of the Italy places we were in.

B: Yeah I did actually.

A: And I was impressed by them as well because I thought Venice I wanted to go but I thought it's gonna stink and be dirty and rubbish somehow

B: Mm. I just thought

A: And too touristy.

B: Yeah. I just thought it'd be like Majorca or Greece type place

A: Yeah

B: But I don't think it was.

A: No. Like we when we got up early and went for a walk over the bridges

B: Yeah.

A: And just let ourselves get lost it was lovely.

B: It was really nice.

A: And when we did get lost but not on purpose it was nice though.

B: Yeah.

A: We've saw all the back streets and it was all the same and little tiny

B: Yeah. Boats and lovely rivers.

A: Windy canals and stuff. Yeah.

B: And I loved the Grand. You know when we went to that big square.

A: The Saint Mark's Square?

B: Yeah.

A: Yeah.

A: And the erm was it Palace Du Car or something like that?

B: Yeah. We we did the Basilica

A: Cos it was the main thing.

B: Yeah. Oh yeah

A: And then we did that palace

B: That was amazing

A: And we did Bridge Of Sighs.

B: Yeah.

A: And then we went at night. I loved that and there was all the string quartets and everything. That was really good.

B: Oh yeah. That was really fantastic

A: That was brilliant

B: That wasn't it?

A: Yeah. I really liked that.

B: That was really good.

A: They were like setting each other off and stuff.

B: Yeah. That was really brilliant.

A: Mm. Yeah I was really impressed by Italy I liked it. I'd go back.

Cambridge Spoken Corpus

RESEARCH QUESTION
Analysing narratives

You can extend your understanding by collecting narratives from different sources that are closely aligned to a sense of place. Analyse how the speakers present their experiences, drawing on the topics, concepts and frameworks that you have explored in this chapter.

Here are some websites that you might find useful in terms of data. Each website contains many different types of narrative that you can explore.

- *My Walk to Work NYC* is a blog that captures short narratives from people from various backgrounds in New York: www.cambridge.org/links/escnar6003

- *Humans of New York* is a project run by Brandon Stanton. His website contains a large number of narratives from those living in the city as well as from other countries. There is also a 'series' section that groups narratives together into themes: for example, stories told by prison inmates or refugees: www.cambridge.org/links/escnar6004

- *The Listening Project* is a partnership between the British Broadcasting Corporation (BBC) and the British Library. The project has recordings of conversations between friends or relatives on a variety of subjects. There is a huge amount of material that can be downloaded and listened to both on the BBC and British Library websites: www.cambridge.org/links/escnar6005

- The American website *StoryCorps®* hosts a similar project. You can listen to and read stories told by a wide range of individuals on www.cambridge.org/links/escnar6006

Wider reading

You can find out more about the topics in this chapter by reading the following:

Labov's narrative structure

Labov, W. (1972) *Language in the Inner City: Studies in the Black English Vernacular*. Philadelphia, PA: University of Pennsylvania Press.

Toolan, M. (2001) *Narrative: A Critical Linguistic Introduction* (Second edition). London: Routledge.

Small stories

Georgakopolou, A. (2007) *Small Stories: Interaction and Identities*. Amsterdam: John Benjamins.

Co-constructing narratives

Garcia, A. (2013) *An Introduction to Interaction: Understanding Talk in Formal and Informal Settings*. London: Bloomsbury.

Jones, R. (2016) *Spoken Discourse*. London: Bloomsbury.

Space and place

Crang, M. (1998) *Cultural Geography*. London: Routledge.

Massey, D. (2005) *For Space*. London: Sage.

Chapter 4
Reading narratives

In this chapter you will:

- Understand the use and effects of deixis and deictic shifts in narratives

- Consider how readers make connections between books and reading experiences

- Examine how authors and readers build, maintain and develop characters

4.1 Reading narratives

This chapter is concerned with reading narratives. Whereas the first three chapters introduced some key aspects and concepts related to the study of narrative and explored these in relation to written narratives in Chapter 2 and to spoken narratives in Chapter 3, the focus in this chapter is on how readers track narratives. The chapter begins by exploring the important linguistic concept of deixis, examining how readers reposition themselves when reading stories. Later sections then explore the connections that readers make between texts and examine how readers build models of characters, events and narrators in their minds when they read.

4.2 Deixis and deictic shift theory

4.2.1 Deixis

Readers commonly talk about being immersed in books, often relating their experiences of reading as intense and memorable and potentially life-changing: reading fiction can often have a stronger impact on individuals than a real-life experience, particularly when the stories are engaging, interesting and relevant, and where tellability is high. An easy way to see evidence of this type of response is to explore the endorsements and reviews that accompany blurbs on the jacket and inner sleeve of a book. You could also look at sites like goodreads. com or reviews on Amazon or other online booksellers to see how readers write about the intense experiences that they have with books.

The psychologist Richard Gerrig (1993) has studied the way that readers reflect on these types of immersive experience. He notes that readers generally talk about what reading feels like to them by using a metaphor of transportation. In this metaphor, the reader describes themselves as a traveller setting forward on a journey into another country (the fictional world of the book). On putting down the book/leaving that country, the reader returns a changed person, having been affected by the journey in some way. As an example of this, read Text 4A, an extract from goodreads.com where a poster reflects on how she felt after reading Colleen Hoover's novel *It Ends With Us*.

Text 4A

> *It Ends With Us* is one of those books that you will remember. You will reach the end of the book and put it down. Yet, thoughts of this book, the characters and the message will continue to linger on your mind for days after you finish, maybe even weeks.

Narrative

It is interesting that the poster frames her reading experience using the metaphor that Gerrig suggests often typifies individuals talking about their reading. Like a journey, she talks of reaching 'the end' and coming away from the experience with intense memories and emotions that will stay with her for some time.

Gerrig develops his ideas on the READING IS TRANSPORTATION metaphor by pointing out that reading a book necessarily involves being distracted from whatever is happening in the 'real world'. That is, when readers enter the world of the story, they get lost in it so far as they immerse themselves within the fictional events of the novel, poem or play that they are reading. Readers therefore project themselves into a story, identifying with its protagonists and experiencing the protagonists' emotions; the reader's response in Text 4A again shows evidence of this aspect.

In fact, this feeling of readerly immersion can be explained by paying attention to the specific textual expressions that help readers to adopt these different perspectives. This involves paying close attention to a feature of language known as deixis. Deictic expressions are context-bound in so far as their meaning depends on who is using them, where they are using them and when they are using them. In other words, they are expressions that help to position a narrative from a particular vantage point.

A central element of deixis is the concept of the deictic centre. This is the origin of an utterance, which establishes a reference point from which other words can be both projected and understood. Read Text 4B, the opening to Christopher Marlowe's 'The passionate shepherd to his love', and Text 4C, the opening to William Stanley Merwin's 'When you go away'.

KEY TERMS

Deixis: words that are context-bound and whose meaning depends on who is using them, and where and when they are being used

Deictic centre: the origin of an expression from which the expression points out and is understood

---

Text 4B

Come live with me and be my Love,

And we will all the pleasures prove

That hills and valleys, dale and field,

And all the craggy mountains yield

Extract from 'The passionate shepherd to his love',
Christopher Marlowe

Text 4C

When you go away the wind clicks around to the north

The painters work all day but at sundown the paint falls

Showing the black walls

The clock goes back to striking the same hour

That has no place in the years

Extract from 'When you go away', William Stanley Merwin (1967)

The deictic centre is a useful concept because it is possible to see how other words and phrases operate in relation to it. In both poems above, the speaking persona projects from a distinctive deictic centre and talks to their addressee using a specific verb which is understood relative to the origin of the utterance. In fact, both verbs can be understood in terms of how they point in relation to the speaker. In Text 4B, the speaker uses the verb 'come' to place the desired movement of the addressee *towards* him; in contrast, in Text 4C, the verb 'go' shows that the addressee is *moving away* from the speaker. These verbs illustrate the basic relationship between a deictic expression and its deictic centre.

Of course, the meaning of a deictic expression will vary depending on who is speaking and the time and the place within which speaking takes place. For example, if someone says the words 'I am here today' sitting in Birmingham on 27 February 2017, the deictic centre consists of a person (the speaker), place (Birmingham) and time (27 February 2017). But, if the same person says those words in a different place and at a different time, then the words 'here' and 'today' will refer to a different place and time zones. If someone else says these words, then the time and place to which they refer will differ again, and so on.

Deictic terms belong to one of a number of categories. The three main categories are:

- **person deixis** (e.g. names and personal pronouns)

- **spatial deixis** (e.g. adverbs of place such as 'here', 'there', demonstratives showing location such as 'this' and 'that', and deictic verbs such as 'come' and 'go')

- **temporal deixis** (e.g. temporal adverbs such as 'today', 'yesterday' and 'tomorrow', and prepositional phrases such as 'in two hours', 'in two weeks' time')

Deictic expressions can also signal degrees of proximity. In the temporal deixis example, 'today' is temporally close to the speaker while 'tomorrow' is more distant. Since deictic terms point outwards from a deictic centre, the concept of closeness is a useful one in distinguishing between deictic terms across all three categories. For example, it is possible to also distinguish between the proximal and distal deictic pairs 'here' and 'now', 'this' and 'that', and 'these and those'.

Figure 4.1 summarises and shows the relationship between these expressions.

Figure 4.1: Categories of deixis

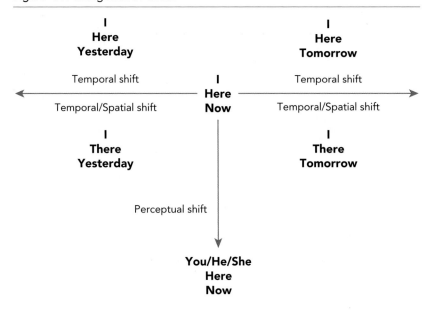

4.2.2 Deictic shifts

So far, you have explored the notion of deixis and looked at the ways that deictic expressions work to position a text relative to its deictic centre. In fact, this anchoring aspect is a particular feature of deixis. You will explore this in more detail in the forthcoming section, specifically focusing on how authors and narrators can manipulate deictic terms so as to give the impression of movement across a text.

Read Text 4D, the opening of Deborah Levy's novel *Hot Milk*.

Text 4D

2015. Almeira. Southern Spain. August.

Today I dropped my laptop on the concrete floor of a bar built on the beach.

Extract from Hot Milk, Deborah Levy, Hamish Hamilton (2016)

In this text, the deictic parameters of the novel are established in the following way.

- **Time:** through the use of the adverb 'Today', nouns '2015' and 'August', and the use of the past tense 'dropped'.

- **Location:** through the use of the proper noun 'Almeira', the pre-modified noun phrase 'Southern Spain' and a series of embedded prepositional phrases 'on the concrete floor of a bar [...] on the beach'.

- **Narrative perspective:** through the use of the first-person pronoun 'I'.

As you saw in Chapter 1, it is possible to distinguish between different levels of telling to examine the effects of an author adopting a particular point of view when narrating. Readers also have to assume a particular point of view or perspective: in the opening of the novel *Hot Milk*, a reader needs to move from their own position (i.e. as a real-world living person) to that of the narrator, in this instance positioning themselves mentally to accept that the 'I' of a narrative refers to the narrator. In other words, readers adopt the deictic centre projected by the use of the pronoun 'I'.

As they read a text the reader generally assumes, unless specifically told otherwise, that the deictic parameters will remain constant. For example, when continuing to read *Hot Milk*, the reader will think that the narrative is still taking place in 2015 in Almeira. And, unless a change in perspective is signalled, they assume that the narrator (Sofia) continues to tell the story. In fact there are specific textual cues that help the reader to keep track of these various deictic fields. You can see this by looking at Text 4E, which is the next section of *Hot Milk*.

Text 4E

It was tucked under my arm and slid out of its black rubber sheath (designed like an envelope), landing screen side down. The digital page is now shattered but at least it still works. My laptop has all my life in it and knows more about me than anyone else.

So what I am saying is that if it is broken, so am I.

Extract from Hot Milk, Deborah Levy, Hamish Hamilton (2016)

The point of view here remains constant. The reader can see this through the continued use of the first-person pronouns 'I' and 'me' as well as the possessive determiner 'my' that maintain the focus on Sofia as the narrator. The time frame is also maintained initially through the use of the verb phrases 'was tucked' and 'slid' that highlight events in the recent past. However, the adverb 'now' and the shift to present tense verbs anchor the narrative more clearly in the present. And, there is no indication of any change in location (simply because the location is not commented on!) so the reader assumes that Sofia is still in Almeira.

Alternatively, authors can change these parameters by asking the reader to shift between particular deictic fields, from one perceptual, temporal or spatial centre to another as they read. This results in a deictic shift (Segal 1995). For example, the narrative viewpoint might switch to another character or flashback to a memory in a previous time frame. Or the location in which the narrative events occur might change so that the action is presented as taking place somewhere else. In these instances, the reader must now re-imagine a new scene and read on from that point in relation to this new deictic centre.

KEY TERM

Deictic shift: a movement between particular deictic fields, from one perceptual, temporal or spatial centre to another

---

It is possible to distinguish between words and phrases that function to shift the deictic centre and those that are anti-shift devices, with the default assumption that unless told otherwise, a deictic centre will remain as it is. Common shifting and anti-shifting devices in each of the categories of deixis are in Table 4.1.

Table 4.1: Categories of deixis

Type of deixis	Shifting devices	Anti-shifting devices
Person deixis	Use of a new character/ narrator's name	Repetition of a character's name or continued reference through the use of a pronoun
Spatial deixis	Verbs of movement and prepositions that point to a new location	Repetition of a place or location name, added description of it, or the use of adverbs 'here' and 'there' to maintain the focus
Temporal deixis	Use of a different verb tense, use of adverbials such as 'back then' to emphasise a different time frame, the explicit mentioning of another year, day or time	Maintaining tense or the use of the adverb 'now' to emphasis the focus on the current time frame

ACTIVITY 4.1
Exploring deictic shifts in poetry
Read Text 4F, one section of Andrew Motion's long poem 'Anniversaries'. What do you notice about deixis and any deictic shifts in this poem? How do these features help you to understand and interpret the poem?

Text 4F

The first

What I remember is not

your leaving, but your not

coming back – and snow

creaking in thick trees,

burying tracks preserved

in spiky grass below.

All afternoon I watched

from the kitchen window

a tap thaw in the yard,

oozing into its stiff sack,

then harden when evening

closed with ice again.

And I am still there,

seeing your horse return

alone to the open stable,

its reins dragging behind

a trail across the plough,

a blurred riddle of scars

we could not decipher then,

and cannot heal now.

Extract from 'Anniversaries', Andrew Motion (1998)

4.3 Intertextuality

The term intertextuality is used to refer to the connections that exist between different texts. This may be when an episode or reference in one text explicitly draws on some aspect of another. For example, the American television shows *The Simpsons* and *Stranger Things* frequently make reference to events and characters from other texts. And, Simon Armitage's poem 'Kid' draws extensively on the television programme/comic book relationship between the characters Batman and Robin in order to present its themes.

Sometimes, one text might be partly, or nearly wholly, dependent on another such as in the case of prequels or sequels, or when a number of references in one depend on a reader having read the other. For example, Tom Stoppard's play *Rosencrantz and Guildenstern are Dead* (1966) takes two minor characters from Shakespeare's *Hamlet* and reconfigures parts of the original play from their perspective. Arguably, to understand Stoppard's play, it is necessary to have at least some basic knowledge of Shakespeare's.

Equally, some postmodern literature is heavily intertextual. Paul Auster's *The New York Trilogy* (1990) consists of three detective stories that invite the reader to make connections between them. This is both indirectly through common plots and themes and more explicitly through characterisation. For example, Quinn, a writer who mistakenly gets hired as a private detective, is the main protagonist of the first story, *City of Glass*. He later reappears in the final story, *The Locked Room*, again in the role of a private detective but this time serving on a different case. The reference to Quinn here forces the reader to both re-evaluate the events of the first story as well as question Quinn's role in the later one.

An alternative way, however, of understanding intertextuality is to view it as a mental rather than a text-based phenomenon. That is, readers themselves make connections between texts regardless of whether those connections are explicitly foregrounded. Some researchers refer to this as *accidental intertextuality* to highlight the fact that there is no perceived authorial intention behind the connection. However, it can be argued that the notion of downplays the role of the reader and their experiences and memories in making meaning through drawing on their own resources. As you have seen in previous chapters, the careful shaping of different kinds of stories by writers (and speakers) and the emotional responses of readers (and listeners) to them is strong evidence that narratives are highly personal experiences.

The stylistician Jessica Mason (2014) argues that for this reason intertextuality ought to be thought of as a cognitive phenomenon. In doing so, linguists can look for ways in which readers draw on different kinds of narratives as they talk about their reading and tell stories. Mason uses the notion of a schema to explain how readers store and use various kinds of information about their reading.

A schema is a bundle of knowledge that an individual holds about some relevant concept, entity or experience. For example, anyone who has travelled by air will have an 'airport' schema that they would use to help them know what to do when they travel: get to the airport; check in; go through security; go shopping; go to departures lounge, and so on. Schemas develop and change through experience: travellers' knowledge of airports will become more fine-tuned and expert the more they fly and may develop to include more specialist, idiosyncratic aspects of knowledge. For example, most airlines now offer online check in and airports in different parts of the world may have set-ups that are unique to them. If someone travels to a particular airport where there are no shops, they will keep this information in mind if they use that same airport again and not be disappointed that they can't spend their money!

Schemas can be shared by groups of people but essentially a schema is personal and largely unique to an individual. This is because schemas are not only developed from what is experienced but also from what is read and talked about. For example, an individual's 'airport' schema may also be informed from watching television programmes about airports or seeing photographs on the internet or listening to a family member talking about their own experience.

Mason argues that readers will have a narrative schema for each book they have read. This will be based on their own reading of the book and on other aspects such as where they read it, for example at school or at the beach, the age they were and what else they were doing in their life at the time. Equally – and amazingly – a reader will often have narrative schemas about books that they have never read. For example, I have never read Victor Hugo's *Notre-Dame de Paris* (better known in English as *The Hunchback of Notre Dame*) but I know the story, the names of the characters and can even picture key scenes in my mind. This is largely because the novel has been widely quoted and adapted: I have seen film versions and children's cartoons based on the story, and the characters of Quasimodo and Esmeralda have formed part of a variety of popular culture media. In fact, I have heard people talking about it so often and feel so familiar with the novel that I have never felt it necessary to read it myself.

KEY TERMS

Intertextuality: a process by which texts borrow from or refer to the content or conventions of other texts

Schema: a bundle of information about something held in the mind

Narrative schema: an individual's mental version of a particular narrative

4 Narrative

Readers draw on narrative schemas as they read, think and, crucially, talk about their experiences with books. The narratives they draw on may be non-fictional episodes from their life as well as other books. Text 4G is taken from the customer review section on Amazon. The reviewer is an adult writing about *First Term at Malory Towers* by the children's author Enid Blyton.

Text 4G

Ah, how much did I love these books when I was a kid? I so desperately wanted to be friends with Darrell Rivers et al and tip-toe down to the beach for midnight feasts with lashings and lashings of ginger beer!

I must have read the whole series at least 10 times, and I recently rediscovered them when I was off work sick for a few days – I curled up under my duvet with mugs of lemsip and lost myself in the best boarding school in the world for a few days. I'm in my 30's [sic] now (well into them, but shhh!) and I could have been a 10 year old again, they made me feel carefree and happy.

The series follows Darrell Rivers and friends (Sally, Mary Lou etc) through their 5 years at boarding school on the Cornish coast and we meet and fall in love with an array of fabulous characters along the way including spoilt, sulky Gwendoline, headstrong Alicia and tomboy Bobbie.

I just loved these books years ago and I still love them now. Whether you have never read any Mallory [sic] Towers or you grew up with them like me, then you are about to get a real treat by picking this book up. Enjoy.

In this review, the writer makes connections between several narratives. She draws on the Enid Blyton novel but interweaves a story about being sick and off work, being reminded of herself as a young girl as she was re-reading and generally remarks on growing up with Enid Blyton's writing. Overall, her talk demonstrates that she has a narrative schema for *Malory Towers* that is continuing to be enriched and developed even as an adult.

ACTIVITY 4.2
Narrative schemas

Put together a small corpus of reader reviews from goodreads.com and Amazon to explore how readers talk about their reading and how they draw on other narratives to make connections. You could explore how adults write about children's or young adult fiction. To what extent do they reminisce about their childhood and make sense of their reading in the light of both adult and remembered child experiences?

4.4 Reading characters

4.4.1 A model of characterisation

The way that readers of narratives respond to, understand and track characters across a text is part of the process of characterisation. Characterisation may refer to the particular strategies that an author uses to present characters over time but crucially it also refers to the strategies that readers use as they build up rich representations of character from what they read. With this in mind, the final two sections of this chapter return to the concept of the schema.

> ### KEY TERM
> **Characterisation:** the range of strategies authors and readers use to build, maintain and develop characters

Reading a novel or poem involves both drawing on a range of knowledge from outside of the text and responding to individual words and phrases within it. As you saw in section 4.3, knowledge is stored in structures called schemas. These are triggered by specific details in the text and help the reader construct a coherent narrative. Consequently, much of the fleshing out of a story relies on the schemas that a reader holds.

There are two important points here that are worth further discussion. First, although readers will share many aspects of knowledge, schemas are essentially personal; that is, one person's schema will always be at least slightly different to another's. Taking the example of the 'airport' schema explored in the previous section, there will clearly be differences in schemas depending on the type of airports an individual has visited, the frequency of travel, and so on. Second, it is important to acknowledge that readers rely on two kinds of knowledge: schemas that are built up from experiences in and understanding of the 'real' world and those which are effectively developed from within the fictional world, including the events and characters introduced within it by the author.

As an example of how these two kinds of knowledge work, read Text 4H, the opening to Ottessa Moshfegh's novel *Eileen*.

Text 4H

> I looked like a girl you'd expect to see on a city bus, reading some clothbound book from the library about plants or geography, perhaps wearing a net over my light brown hair. You might take me for a nursing student or a typist, note the nervous hands, a foot tapping, bitten lip.
>
> Extract from *Eileen*, Ottessa Moshfegh, Vintage (2016)

This text contains words and phrases, or textual cues, that trigger schemas. At a basic level, the noun 'girl' triggers a 'person' schema, which is used to provide a basic platform from which the narrative is understood. For example, a reader might flesh out the details provided in the text to determine that the narrator is travelling as she needs to get somewhere, based on a 'journey' schema. And the specific reference to the fact that she is a 'girl', as opposed to a 'human' or a 'woman', might trigger a specific image of what the girl looks like and is feeling in the reader's mind (you'll explore this aspect a little more in section 4.4.2). As the reader continues to read, individual words also rely on background knowledge to build up a mental picture of the events in the narrative. For example, initially 'city bus' might trigger different associative memories in different readers, depending on the type of city they live in, what size and colour the buses are there, and so on. Equally, the narrator's suggestion that she might be seen as a 'nursing student' or a 'typist' relies on a considerable amount of reader background knowledge to create a mental image. Again, there are degrees to which a reader might be able to imagine how old a typical nursing student or typist might be, what she might look like and what she might be doing.

KEY TERM

Textual cue: a word or phrase that triggers a reader drawing on a schema

However, there is also a schema internal to the narrative that is gradually built up. Although a reader may already have a narrative schema for Eileen that has been built up from hearing about the book from friends or even reading the blurb on the back cover, the initial interaction with the text enriches their narrative schema considerably. In the text, the initial 'character' schema triggered by the word 'girl' is modified by explicit textual detail in the noun phrases 'light brown hair', 'the nervous hands', 'a foot tapping', and 'bitten lip'. This shows how important the words of the text are in developing a 'character' schema as reading progresses. This fictional knowledge is of course dynamic and evolves as the narrative is read. So, the reader's knowledge of Eileen, the places she lives in and visits and the events she takes part in is built up over successive mentions and episodes as the novel is read.

Overall then, characterisation is a combination of two processes: top-down (schemas) and bottom-up (words and phrases in the text), as shown in Figure 4.2.

Figure 4.2: Processes of characterisation

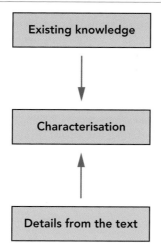

4.4.2 Mind-modelling

As the reader processes and tracks characters in a narrative, they are also building up a picture of the character's mind as they understand it. In fact, studies of characterisation in some areas of literary studies work from the premise that readers effectively view and treat fictional characters as though they were real people. You can see evidence of this in how readers talk powerfully and emotionally about their favourite character in a book and, in extreme circumstances, why some television viewers get upset when their favourite soap opera character 'dies', even though of course the character is not real and the actor playing the part is still very much alive. Indeed the American soap opera *Dallas* once famously brought one of its central characters, Bobby Ewing, back from the dead due to viewer demand, presenting the events surrounding his death as merely a dream. In a similar way, the UK soap *EastEnders* resurrected an old villain, Den Watts (Dirty Den), in order to revive an old storyline and increase ratings.

The stylistician Peter Stockwell (2009) uses the term mind-modelling to describe how generally we try to develop a sense of how others' minds operate. This is the case regardless of whether the person whose mind we are modelling is real or not. In the case of fictional minds, we effectively construct a mind for someone who does not exist!

Stockwell argues that we mind-model using our own experiences and feelings to guide us: in effect, we are the examples of how a mind operates and we use this knowledge to assume that other minds will operate in similar ways. The crucial point here therefore is that we do not start from scratch when building up a character but rather we use an existing template (ourselves) that we further develop and shape as we read. As you saw with Text 4H this means that characterisation is a creative process. As we model a mind, we are to all intents and purposes developing a sense of a character's mind style (see Chapter 2). The notion of mind-modelling also explains how we can attach emotions to characters based on what they say or do, or have done to them. For example, you probably know from your own experience that falling out with a good friend will be a painful and sad experience. If you read about this happening to a character in a novel, you will most likely attribute the same (or some other kind of emotion) to them simply because you know that this is what happens to you. The notion of text-drivenness is important here. Unless the text specifies otherwise, we assume that a character (unless told beforehand that they are an alien!) will be normal to the extent that a reader models them on real-life people they know. Readers may respond to the following cues in order to model the mind of a character:

- what a character looks like

- how they act, speak and think

- how they interact with other characters

- what other characters say about them

- how they present themselves to other characters

- how they present themselves to the reader (if acting as a narrator).

KEY TERMS

Mind-modelling: the process by which readers construct and understand the mind of others

Text-drivenness: the way that readers base their understanding on what is actually specified in the text

To illustrate how a reader might model the mind of a character, read Text 4I, another extract from Moshfegh's *Eileen*, which occurs just after the opening section. In this extract, Eileen reveals to the reader that she is actually an old woman and is looking back on and telling the story of a younger version of herself fifty years earlier.

Text 4I

And back then – this was fifty years ago – I was a prude. Just look at me. I wore heavy wool skirts that fell past my knees, thick stockings. I always buttoned my jackets and blouses as high as they could go. I wasn't a girl who turned heads. But there was nothing really so wrong or terrible about my appearance. I was young and fine, average, I guess. But at the time I thought I was the worst – ugly, disgusting, unfit for the world. In such a state it seemed ridiculous to call attention to myself. I rarely wore jewelry, never perfume, and I didn't paint my nails. For a while I did wear a ring with a little ruby in it. It had belonged to my mother.

Extract from *Eileen*, Ottessa Moshfegh, Vintage (2016)

The manner in which Eileen narrates and reveals aspects of herself to the reader is interesting and helps to shape the sense of her character early on in the novel. As they read, the reader develops a greater sense of Eileen and the largely negative opinion of herself that she has, particularly when she was younger. This is relayed through the negatively-oriented lexis that presents her as unattractive both to herself and to others. There is, however, also an awareness of her own changing mind; the reader gets the sense that Eileen is looking back on a past version of herself and reflecting on that in the context of trying to make sense of the present. In other words, Eileen's mind is an inquiring and self-questioning one.

ACTIVITY 4.3
Characterisation

Choose a short section (around half a page) of a novel that you know well. Think about and try to trace how you develop a sense of character as you read. What impression do you get of the main character or characters? What kinds of textual cues and knowledge do you think you are drawing on to help you make sense of the narrative and model the mind of each character?

Now ask someone else to read the same passage and talk through their response with you. What similarities and differences do you notice? You could repeat this with other readers and look for patterns in how you and they report their responses to this text.

RESEARCH QUESTION
Characters in oral narratives

This chapter has focused on written, and specifically, literary narratives. Can you apply your learning to spoken narratives, drawing on what you studied in Chapter 3? For example, how are characters developed in oral narratives? What strategies do speakers use? How do television/film and radio scripts develop characters given that they have the added benefit of images and/or sound?

Find some examples of spoken narratives and analyse them according to any patterns you find. You could also find some examples of viewers' and listeners' reviews of television or radio programmes and films online and look at how readers talk about their viewing/listening experiences. What can you say about any schemas that they appear to draw on?

Wider reading

You can find out more about the topics in this chapter by reading the following:

Deictic shift theory

Stockwell, P. (2002) *Cognitive Poetics: An Introduction*. London: Routledge.

Intertextuality

Allen, G. (2011) *Intertexuality* (Second edition). London: Routledge.

Mason, J. (2014) 'Narrative' in P. Stockwell and S. Whiteley (eds) *The Cambridge Handbook of Stylistics*. Cambridge: Cambridge University Press, pp.175–94.

Characterisation and mind-modelling

Culpeper, J. (2001) *Language and Characterisation: People in Plays and Other Texts*. Harlow: Longman.

Stockwell, P. (2009) *Texture: A Cognitive Aesthetics of Reading*. Edinburgh: Edinburgh University Press.

Chapter 5
Narrative genres

In this chapter you will:

- Explore the structure of hard news stories and how metaphors are used to underpin narratives

- Explore some of the characteristics of narratives spoken and written by children

- Understand how narratives are constructed on the social media platform Twitter

5.1 Narrative and the news

5.1.1 Hard news

In this section, you will examine some examples of how narrative events are reported in news journalism. The chapter begins by examining an example of a hard news story. According to Allan Bell (1991), this type of story reports on an event which has occurred since the previous issue of the paper. Bell of course was writing before the advent of the internet which has meant that papers can now update their stories very easily and quickly. However, breaking news remains big news and reports will tend to present their narratives in a certain way, drawing on particular genre conventions and more idiosyncratic and ideological language choices.

Look at Text 5A, a report that appeared in a UK newspaper.

Text 5A

Liverpool libraries saved after budget boost – for now

Mayor says plans to close four of the city's 13 libraries will be suspended after chancellor's promise of £27m for social care.

Public libraries in Liverpool have been saved from closure after the government promised £27m for adult social care in the city – however, the city's mayor has warned that the decision is a stay of execution, rather than a permanent reprieve for the beleaguered library service.

The £27m injection is Liverpool's share of an extra £2bn promised last week by the chancellor, Philip Hammond, to shore up local councils' social care provision across the country. Four of the city's 13 libraries were due to close, with others to be transferred to community groups, under plans aimed at saving £1.6m. Liverpool mayor Joe Anderson said the cuts were needed to plug a £90m hole in the local authority's budgets over the next three years.

Extract from Danuta Kean (*The Guardian*, 13 March 2017)

In his discussion of hard news stories, Michael Toolan (2001) argues they tend to be organised in the following way:

- a pithy headline that is a simplified version of the lead sentence and which is usually written by a different journalist

- a lead sentence that includes the most tellable aspects of the story

- orientational and complicating action reports that are often not chronological but move backwards and forwards to maintain their relevance to the lead sentence.

This structure is evident in Text 5A. The headline 'Liverpool libraries saved after budget boost – for now' is followed by the lead sentence 'Mayor says plans to close four of the city's 13 libraries will be suspended after chancellor's promise of £27m for social care', which captures the most important – and therefore tellable–parts of the story. The remaining two paragraphs present the main narrative detail but interestingly, and following Toolan's argument, the events are ordered non-chronologically. The narrative events *as they occurred* are:

- four libraries were due to close due to cuts in funding

- Philip Hammond has promised £27m for Liverpool

- the libraries have been saved from closure

- the mayor is warning that this may not be permanent.

The narrative events *as they are reported* are:

- the libraries have been saved from closure

- Philip Hammond has promised £27m for Liverpool

- the mayor is warning that this may not be permanent

- four libraries were due to close due to cuts in funding.

The effect of this particular narrative discourse is to maintain attention on the focus of the lead sentence. The most relevant aspect of the story for the community is the saving of the libraries: this is new and highly tellable news. It is also relevant that the funding has been promised, rather than actually given at this stage. The choice of words suggests a possibility that it might not yet happen. This possibility is evident in the way that the newspaper has reported the story.

Text 5A also demonstrates that producers of news narratives very carefully select the specific language choices they utilise. As discussed, the lexical choice 'promise' has a very different meaning to 'gives'. Equally, at the level of syntax, the reporting of the headline using a passive construction (see Chapter 1) places particular emphasis on the patient 'the libraries' rather than the agent responsible for the act of saving, Philip Hammond and his budget. There would be a clear difference in emphasis if the active form were used. For example, imagine if the headline had read:

Philip Hammond saves Liverpool libraries after budget boost – for now

KEY TERMS

Patient: the entity directly acted on by the verb in an action process

Agent: the entity responsible for carrying out the verb in an action process

Narrative

Interestingly, when Philip Hammond does appear in the lead sentence, he is not named but referred to by his title in 'chancellor's promise'. The action itself is also presented in a nominalised form rather than as part of a verb process occurring over time. It seems as though the newspaper wants to avoid giving Philip Hammond too much credit for this particular action!

You can explore similar representations of events and the effects of particular word choices by looking at Text 5B, Text 5C and Text 5D, three newspaper headlines that covered the news that Nicola Sturgeon, leader of the Scottish Nationalist Party, was planning at the time (March 2017) to push for a second referendum on Scottish independence. This followed the referendum on Great Britain's membership of the European Union in June 2016 when the public voted to leave the union.

Text 5B

Sturgeon ambushes May with second referendum plan

The Times, 14 March 2017

Text 5C

First Minister Nicola Sturgeon hits out at 'not yet elected' Prime Minister Theresa May amid Scottish independence vote row

The Sunday Herald, 14 March 2017

Text 5D

Theresa May's refusal to give an inch has forced Sturgeon's hand

The Guardian, 13 March 2017

Although these headlines all report on the same event, they make use of strikingly different stylistic choices. In Text 5B, Nicola Sturgeon is presented as the agent and placed at the head of the clause for prominence, and followed by the verb 'ambushes' and the patient 'May'. Text 5C also has an agent–verb–patient structure; however this time Nicola Sturgeon is described as the 'First Minister'. It could be argued that this choice emphasises her political position and therefore makes her action appear less personal and more acceptable. If we look at the verb choices, it also becomes apparent that the first headline is less sympathetic towards Nicola Sturgeon. The verb 'ambushes' has strong connotations of violence: to ambush means to attack someone by surprise and is usually used in a military context. *The Times*' representation of Nicola Sturgeon in this instance is that of an aggressor. In contrast, although 'hits out' in Text 5C also portrays a violent action, it suggests that Sturgeon's action is more of a reaction to something that Theresa May has done. This is also supported by the fact that again Theresa May is pre-modified by '"not yet elected" Prime Minister'; the use of the quotation 'not yet elected' arguably again softens and authorises the action Nicola Sturgeon has taken.

It is no surprise that the ways in which these newspapers present events depends on their political outlook. Indeed the language choices they use promote distinctive ways of viewing the world and the ideologies that underpin them. *The Times* has a history of backing Theresa May and was a vocal opponent of Scottish independence. On the other hand, *The Sunday Herald* was one of the few newspapers that supported the independence cause in the first referendum and is known to support Nicola Sturgeon's policies.

Text 5D from *The Guardian* manipulates the structure of the first and reverses the roles within the clause. In Text 5D, agency is given to a nominalised form 'Theresa May's refusal to give an inch' with another noun phrase 'Sturgeon's hand' acting as the patient. Interestingly, neither politician is referenced directly here; instead, they are accessed by their actions. In this example, the verb 'has forced' also firmly positions the blame for Nicola Sturgeon's position with Theresa May. Unsurprisingly, *The Guardian* is known for its lack of sympathy towards the Conservative Party and its criticism of Theresa May as Prime Minister.

5.1.2 Metaphor: politics and ideology

The headlines discussed in the previous section show how news items function as distinctive types of narrative. In fact, the field of politics more generally is interesting to explore in terms of how writers and speakers promote their ideologies and structure their narratives accordingly (see also *Language and Power* in this series). A useful way of exploring political narratives and examining how ideologies underpin texts involves looking at how metaphors are used as structuring devices.

Metaphors work by presenting abstract concepts in terms of more physical ones. For example, the conceptual metaphor LIFE IS A JOURNEY presents one domain of knowledge in terms of another. Here, the concept of 'life' is the source domain, which provides a structure for understanding the target domain, the more abstract notion of 'journey'. Thus aspects of a journey, such as deciding on a destination, how far we travel and difficulties faced in reaching an end point are used to structure experiences in our lives. Indeed when we talk about our lives, we often draw on the same language as when we talk about journeys, for example 'I've reached a crossroads in my career', 'my life is really going places', and so on.

KEY TERMS

Conceptual metaphor: a structure that presents one concept in terms of another

Source domain: a domain of knowledge used to understand another concept (target domain)

Target domain: the concept that is understood through another domain of knowledge (source domain)

Narrative

Politicians frequently draw on metaphors and use them in their narratives so as to construct a sense of reality that appears to be plausible to those they are addressing. Indeed Jonathan Charteris-Black (2014) argues that the use of metaphor is a defining feature of any politician's speech. In other words metaphors are an essential tool for representing ideas and projecting a certain way of viewing the world.

To explore this idea in more detail, read Text 5E. This is an extract from a speech given in September 2013 by the then Conservative Party UK Chancellor of the Exchequer, George Osborne.

Text 5E

Many risks remain. These are still the early stages of recovery.

But we mustn't go back to square one.

We mustn't lose what the British people have achieved.

This is a hard, difficult road we have been following.

But it is the only way to deliver a sustained, lasting improvement in the living standards of the families of this country.

Extract from speech by George Osborne (Chancellor of the Exchequer, 2013)

In this speech, Osborne uses a number of metaphors to provide a structure for his ideas. These are as follows:

- THE COUNTRY IS A PATIENT: the UK is seen as being in the 'early stages of recovery' from the illness of the last government.

- POLITICS IS A JOURNEY: Osborne uses the concept of 'a road' and the larger source domain of a journey to conceptualise both politics and the UK people travelling with the government towards a better future.

- the orientational metaphors FORWARDS IS GOOD; BACKWARDS IS BAD are used by Osborne to explicitly warn against the dangers faced and how the government will ensure their plan of action will be best for the country.

- ACHIEVEMENTS ARE OBJECTS: Osborne argues that these can be lost but that his party will ensure that this does not happen. Instead the Chancellor promises that the Conservative Party will deliver achievements to the people.

These metaphors are used to position the audience to buy into the 'reality' that Osborne promotes and to view the world in the terms he suggests. Of course, an audience can either choose to share this version of reality or read critically against it. And, as a student of English language, you can uncover the ideologies that inform it so as to make them visible and critically examine them by undertaking this type of critical discourse analysis.

KEY TERM

Critical discourse analysis: an approach to exploring texts that focuses on how power and ideologies are established and presented through language

---

ACTIVITY 5.1

Analysing metaphor

Read Text 5F, an extract from President Donald Trump's US inauguration speech in January 2017. Identify the metaphors that Trump uses and explain how these might promote a particular view of the world. How does Trump draw on particular source domains to construct his narrative?

Text 5F

We must protect our borders from the ravages of other countries making our products, stealing our companies, and destroying our jobs. Protection will lead to great prosperity and strength.

I will fight for you with every breath in my body – and I will never, ever let you down.

America will start winning again, winning like never before.

We will bring back our jobs. We will bring back our borders. We will bring back our wealth. And we will bring back our dreams.

We will build new roads, and highways, and bridges, and airports, and tunnels, and railways all across our wonderful nation.

We will get our people off of welfare and back to work – rebuilding our country with American hands and American labor.

Extract from Donald Trump's inauguration speech (January 2017)

5.2 Children's narratives

5.2.1 Children as narrators

In this section, you will examine narratives written by children. This section continues to broaden out the notion of a narrative to think about the types of speaking and writing young people might engage in. It explores a number of ways that young people shape story content in order to represent themselves and their experiences.

Largely, children may be defined as being novice rather than expert writers. The terms 'novice' and 'expert' were originally coined by Maryanne Wolf (2007) to describe children as readers and may be thought of as two ends of a continuum rather than as a binary pair. As relative novices, children are distinct from adults in the ways they see the world, and in terms of their life experiences and linguistic skills.

> ### KEY TERMS
> **Novice writer**: a writer with limited technical awareness and skill
>
> **Expert writer**: a writer with developed technical awareness and skill

5.2.2 Beginning to narrate

The ability to tell stories is something that emerges gradually in young children. Simple narrative events are easy to put together but children are also faced with the challenge of thinking about ways of personalising their stories and making them tellable. Think back to the distinction made in Chapter 1 between *story* and *narrative discourse*. It is the act of shaping a story that is the biggest challenge for a young person. Eve V. Clark (2016) argues that oral storytelling as a form requires a greater mastery and set of skills than everyday conversation for this very reason. Clark suggests that to develop as storytellers, children need to have awareness of three things:

- **Structural options:** for example, the different ways in which events can be presented in the active and passive voice or by moving elements around in a clause.

- **Rhetorical options:** for example, story openings and closings, the use of evaluations to add tension and present a personal perspective, the use of prosodic features such as intonation, speed and volume to support the narrative and engage the listener.

- **Discursive options:** for example, the choice of formal or informal words and phrases.

In addition, Clark argues that young narrators need to show an awareness of their audience and how they are tracking their stories, making changes and adapting their narrative as needs be – all in all a complex process!

Of course, children develop these skills as they become more experienced with narrative form. For example, read Text 5G. This is a short narrative spoken by Anna, who was five and a half years old at the time.

Text 5G

> Once upon a time in a dark dark dark dark woods, there lived a hideous beast and do you know what the hideous beast was called? The tree monster! And the tree monster was so hideous that no one could look at him. So one night when it was midnight the tree monster came out and the tree monster said to the little girl 'Are you awake?' Then suddenly she woke up and she saw a hideous hand but then it disappeared again. The next midnight, the little girl was still awake, she waited for the hand to come back but as she saw the hand she saw a hideous face and the hideous face was the tree monster! But then the tree monster went away!

In this narrative, Anna shows that she is developing her narrative skills. She makes use of structural features such as the story opening, 'Once upon a time', pre-modified noun phrases such as 'dark dark dark dark woods' and 'hideous hand' to add descriptive detail and, in Labov's terms, provides both an orientation and a complicating action. The ending is weaker with little sense of the narrative being resolved but this is largely sacrificed for the more dramatic moments when she tries to engage her audience. She does this through the use of direct speech, questions and exclamative sentences. In addition, she shows some command of discursive options available to her, including the use of particular lexical choices for effect such as the repeated adjectives 'dark' and 'hideous'. The narrative is also informed by an understanding of generic conventions. Anna attempts to provide a story that is mysterious and scary; in fact, in this instance she was drawing heavily on her own reading of children's books such as *The Ghost Train* (Ahlberg and Amstutz) and *Creaky Castle* (Clarke and Fox), which both tell stories in similar ways.

Generally, the older children get, the greater their ability to work within these options increases. Indeed there is a substantial amount of research that argues that children's writing develops in stages. For example, Jean Rothery and Jim Martin (1980) suggest that there is a standard order in which children acquire mastery of genres of writing. They argue that children's narrative writing (they also propose that children develop a non-narrative or expository style) develops as indicated in Table 5.1. In common with all so-called stage theories, it is important to remember that there will always be exceptions and it is not possible to generalise across all children in all contexts.

Table 5.1: Development of writing genres (adapted from Rothery and Martin, 1980)

Age	Type of narrative	Details
2–4	Observation and comment	Simple points made about the world
5	Recount	A series of events linked together
9	Personal narrative	A narrative in the sense proposed by Labov including orientation, complicating action and resolution but based on personal experience
12	Vicarious narrative	A narrative in the sense proposed by Labov including orientation, complicating action and resolution but moving away from personal experience with less reliance on images and a more mature sense of readership (for example, beyond writing simply for the child's teacher)
15	Thematic narrative	A narrative that serves to make a larger point about the world, acting as an interpretation of what the writer sees which is shaped through narrative, e.g. literary writing

5.2.3 An asset-based approach

Think about the development of writing in more detail by looking at Text 5H. This extract is taken from research by Lorna Bourke and Anne-Marie Adams (2010).

Text 5H

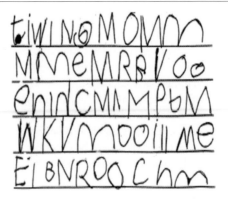

On first reading, it will probably be impossible for you to make much, if any, sense of this. Although some of the marks appear to be similar to letters in the English alphabet, there is little sense that these have been put together in a coherent way. However, now read Text 5L, the transliteration.

Text 5I

I play with my friends. I open the door. I played out. I played hopscotch. I played with my friends.

It should now be evident that this narrative has a clear structure and progresses logically from one event to another. The writer intends to communicate a message and is able to recount her experiences and events in a structured way so that they make sense. In fact this is an example of what might be called emergent writing; the child here understands that writing is a tool or resource with which she is able to communicate, and understands that there is some relationship between the spoken language she uses and the physical marks she has placed on the page. (For more on how children learn to write, see Chapter 4 in *Language Development* in this series.)

Seeing the positive in Text 5I is adopting what is known as an asset-based approach to children's narrative skills. Indeed, an asset-based approach calls into question the whole nature of literacy itself. For example, researchers working within the area of study known as multiple literacies argue that we take part in many different types of reading and writing activities or literacy events in our daily lives. And, literacy events, and the values attached to them, will vary from culture to culture. For example, in a famous study, the American sociolinguist Shirley Brice Heath (1983) undertook an ethnographic study of two working-class communities in the Piedmont Carolinas in the USA over a nine-year period. One of the communities, Trackton, had a largely black population and the other, Roadville, had a white population. She found that, although both communities valued storytelling, the stories in each served different functions. In Roadville, stories tended to be factual and were used to promote clear moral messages whilst in Trackton there was less concern with retelling facts and more value attached to being creative and imaginative, even if this strayed from the truth. Although the communities were only six miles apart, they had very different ideas about what storytelling should be and drew on different resources.

Equally, Kate Pahl (2007) argues that children's literacy practices draw on their different domains of life. A domain is a practice or a type of cultural experience that a child might be engaged in at home that they then use in formal educational settings when they are asked to write. As Pahl suggests:

> Children experience the same ritual practices time after time, such as the ritual of giving presents or playing games, and this ritual is reflected in their drawings and writing. Children's identities are drawn from home, where they learn ways of being and doing and these ways of being and doing are brought to school. (Pahl 2007: 86)

KEY TERMS

Emergent writing: rudimentary writing that nonetheless shows evidence that a child understands that marks on a page communicate a message

Literacy event: an occasion where an individual engages in a form of reading or writing

When examining children's written narratives then, it is useful to think about what they can do and identify the competencies that they display as well as any obvious errors: this after all is a sign of a developing writer.

ACTIVITY 5.2
Zara's writing

To explore the characteristics of a young child's narrative in more detail, read Text 5J. This is an example of a piece of independent writing by four-year-old Zara, inspired by watching the film *The Snowman* and completed at school. What competencies does Zara show and how does she present her narrative?

Text 5J

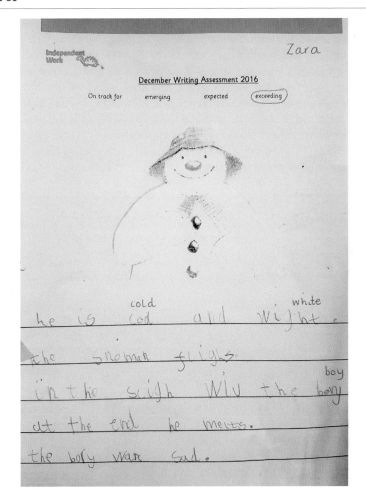

Transliteration

He is cold and white. The snowman flies in the sky with the boy. At the end he melts. The boy was sad.

5.3 Narrative and Twitter

5.3.1 Discourse features

Twitter is a micro-blogging platform that allows users to post short messages, known as tweets, about themselves, follow other users, and share and embed tweets that others have made. Founded in 2006, by early 2017 it had 319 million monthly active users sending 500 million tweets per day. Communication between users may be either synchronous, asynchronous or a combination of both.

Twitter has some very distinctive discourse and language features which impact on the kinds of narratives that users are able to tell. First, users will choose a username and sometimes an avatar so as to project an identity. Some users (especially celebrities using the platform to raise their status) will use their own name but many users will use a different name. Individuals may also include links to other social media platforms, personal websites and blogs. In this way, users consciously construct and project an identity for themselves in the same way as they would in off-line discourse. Consequently, their acts of storytelling become a way of further projecting this identity.

KEY TERMS

Synchronous: communication that takes place in real time and in a continuous exchange

Asynchronous: communication where users do not post to each other in real time

Username: the online name assumed by a user

Avatar: an image-based representation of a user that accompanies a username

Twitter has a limitation of 140 characters per tweet. Clearly this constrains the types of stories that individuals can tell. This restriction also means that users tend to narrate in short bursts of multiple tweets rather than in a long single stretch that would form a spoken or conventional written narrative. These stories also tend to focus on the 'here' and 'now' and can appear fragmentary and move between narration and evaluation in a way that is more subtle than conventional spoken language. For example read Text 5K, a series of tweets that were posted over a ten-minute sequence. In this set of tweets, the narrator moves between providing her opinion on English teaching and telling a story about her own son's problem at school. Arguably, the constraints of the medium, as well as her strong feelings, result in how the bulk of the narration (tweets 3 and 4) is framed by extensive evaluative comment.

Text 5K

> 1 excellent article. As parent of primary age children but also stylistics student…
>
> 2 I get worried about how Eng taught to my kids. 9yo gets really stressed abt…
>
> 3 fronted adverbials and subordinate clauses. I got to chat to him and finally…
>
> 4 managed to explain that they're all just tools to help him understand text which…
>
> 5 Really helped him. But is clearly not being taught so how many kids just don't…
>
> 6 WHY they are being crammed with stuff that basically seems irrelevant and difficult to them? So sorry about multiple tweets, just a subject close to me.

5.3.2 Co-constructed narration

One of the affordances of Twitter is that it makes co-constructed narratives possible. One way that users can do this is through sharing another user's tweet, known as retweeting. In effect, retweeting is a type of announcement whereby the retweeter recommends to their followers that another user's post is worth reading for one reason or another. Sometimes high tellability might be revealed through a quoted retweet, as in Text 5L below. However, this is not always a sign of endorsement and sometimes users will make it very clear that retweeting does not indicate that they agree with the contents of a tweet.

Text 5L

> "This looks super"
>
> [[We're really excited to be hosting this *free* English Language Taster Day for A Level students on 15th March. A few places still available]]

Twitter also facilitates the co-construction of narrative by allowing users to embed stories within their tweets that are hosted outside of the site. At the beginning of this chapter, you explored how the headline of a hard news story functioned as a focal point around which the rest of the narrative was structured. Twitter users also commonly use this technique as a way of bringing in additional narrative material.

Narrative

Ruth Page (2013) argues that an original tweet functions as a caption and may introduce the embedded link by functioning in one of three ways that correspond to Labov's narrative elements (see Chapter 3).

1 As an abstract, compressing and summarising an event:

Text 5M

> Football clubs raided in tax scandal – 180 officers involved!
> www.cambridge.org/links/escnar6007

2 As an orientation, providing contextual information that sets the scene so that the link can be understood once opened:

Text 5N

> After a massively successful first novel, what will critics say about her second? Read here
> www.cambridge.org/links/escnar6008

3 As an evaluation, providing a comment that gives the user's attitude towards the event in the link:

Text 5O

> Programme up for what looks like a fantastic 2 days. Looking forward to paper
> www.cambridge.org/links/escnar6009

Interestingly, Page argues that the embedded links may also serve to further project or perform a sense of an identity in so far as they are deliberately chosen and framed within some type of comment by the user. By drawing on a corpus study of tweets by well-known celebrities, Page demonstrates how this type of amplification strategy is a method by which those with a high Twitter profile build up an online identity with the aim of attracting more followers.

5.3.3 Narrative contexts and identities

Finally, it is worth considering the contexts within which narratives constructed on Twitter are produced and received. The term collapsed contexts was coined by danah boyd (2008) to refer to the fact that users' followers form one single online group which may consist of many different offline groups. For example, a user's follower list may bring together friends, work colleagues and people known in other contexts, as well as any celebrities they are following. You can check this by looking at your list of followers (or a friend's if you don't have a Twitter account) and seeing how many different groups of people are brought together in a single follower/following list.

In developing his ideas on how we construct identities for ourselves in different social spaces, Erving Goffman (1959) used the analogy of a stage, by describing its front stage region as a public space where expectations around behaviour were adhered to and its back stage region as a more private space where an individual can be more informal and relaxed. Drawing on this idea, Page (2013) argues that Twitter users face a tension in how they might want to present themselves to a multiple audience, given that these contexts (front and back stage regions) are necessarily collapsed. Page's own research showed that this tension was particularly evident in tweets posed by celebrities who were concerned about how they presented aspects of their private lives on a public forum.

ACTIVITY 5.3

Collapsed contexts

You can explore the notion of collapsed contexts fairly easily by looking at the tweets of a single user. Are there variations in style and content in terms of tweets? Do you get the sense that there are different identities that are being projected?

RESEARCH QUESTION

Investigation

Collect your own corpus of narratives (news reporting, social media or children's narratives) and do some investigative work using ideas covered in this chapter. You could focus on one or more of the following.

- An investigation of how the same hard news story is reported across different publications, examining how readers are positioned to accept a version of narrative events.

- An exploration of the features of children's writing, looking at the resources they draw on and the kinds of narrative techniques they use.

- An examination of how users project identities through their narratives on Twitter, exploring how the affordances and limitations of the platform affect storytelling.

Wider reading

You can find out more about the topics in this chapter by reading the following:

Narrative in the news

Charteris-Black, J. (2014) *Analysing Political Speeches: Rhetoric, Discourse and Metaphor*. Basingstoke: Palgrave Macmillan.

Fairclough, N. (2014) *Language and Power* (Third edition). London: Routledge.

Jeffries, L. (2009) *Critical Stylistics: The Power of English*. Basingstoke: Palgrave Macmillan.

Toolan, M. (2001) *Narrative: A Critical Linguistic Introduction* (Second edition). London: Routledge.

Children's narratives

Gillen, J. (2003) *The Language of Children*. London: Routledge.

The CHILDES project contains a number of corpora of children's narratives that can be analysed: https://childes.talkbank.org

Narrative and social media

Page, R. (2013) *Stories and Social Media: Identities and Interaction*. London: Routledge.

Zappavigna, M. (2013) *Discourse of Twitter and Social Media: How We Use Language to Create Affiliation on The Web*. London: Bloomsbury.

Ideas and answers

Chapter 1

Activity 1.2

Abi Wilkinson represents individuals and groups largely through mentioning their profession or their political leaning. In doing so she draws on well-established ways of conceptualising the characteristics that groups have: for example 'billionaire business magnates' are conventionally seen as self-interested and out of touch with ordinary people. She also draws on oppositions, for example the wealthy versus 'peasants' and adopts a common media strategy of compartmentalising people into 'camps' (here the ideas draw on a military metaphor of groups in physical opposition).

The world-view presented here attempts to move away from a simple binary to portraying the political fallout following the referendum as being more subtle and complicated. There are clearly Discourses (ways of thinking and writing) of politics and journalism here but also an examination of wider Discourses of regionalism (the concern that London is supporting the rest of the UK) and, of course, grand Discourses of nationalism, separation and integration, all of which formed a central part of the referendum campaign for the two sides.

Overall, Wilkinson offers a combination of subjective and objective narration. She often uses the first person pronoun 'I' but equally reverts to a more objective tone in places, using strategies such as questions and quotations, to make her article perhaps sound more general and rational than a straightforward subjective account.

Activity 1.3

One of the most interesting points about this narrative is that it centres on a family member (A's father) and is personal to the speaker, who therefore has a strong motivation for wanting to tell his tale. The fact that the speaker's father was a police officer also increases the tellability of any possible narrative, evident in B's response 'No kidding?'

The stories that A begins to tell are prompted by B's questions: '… big things that have been on the news … ?' and 'Any major?'. These again provide a frame within which any narrative that follows is likely to be highly exciting, unusual and thus tellable. Indeed, the beginning of A's story that follows (involving the arrest of some bikers in San Francisco) offers such a tale. Interestingly, a crucial part of the tellability of this story comes as a result of the interaction between A and B; in effect, tellability is co-constructed between them, creating a space for a memorable narrative (see Chapter 3 for more on how tellability can depend on context and the relationship between speakers).

Chapter 2

Activity 2.2

In this extract, Rachel's potential unreliability is signalled through the fact that she contradicts herself, most notable in her denial of the events that she has just reported: 'This is not actually true' and later 'I have no idea what he was wearing'. This causes the reader to seriously doubt the credibility of any of her narrative. She also admits to memory loss. 'I have a memory of it, but I can't tell whether the memory belongs to Saturday night or to another time', which undermines her trustworthiness as a narrator.

Rachel's narration is full of words and phrases that express degrees of certainty: 'pretty sure', 'think', 'might have', 'it's possible', 'can't tell'. These modalised constructions (read section 2.3 on modality) represent Rachel as having very little sense of the accuracy of what she has witnessed. In addition, her admission that there have been 'many slips, on many staircases' further suggests that she is not to be trusted. The use of the indefinite determiner 'many' implies that Rachel's erratic behaviour means that she cannot be considered to be reliable.

Activity 2.3

Two possible rewritings are given below. Bold indicates the changes, but there are of course many other ways of changing the modality in the extract.

Positively shaded version

I **was definitely** in bed when I heard the gate. I **had** to listen carefully: I wasn't **obliged** to hear anything else. But I **should have** heard that. I **needed** to wake Cliff. He was passed out. So I **made myself** get up and went to the window. A big moon was laid over the mountains that **forced** its way around the city. It was a white moon and it **had** to be covered with scars.

Negatively shaded version

I was in bed – **maybe** – when I **thought** that I heard the gate. I **might have** listened carefully: I **wasn't sure** if I could hear anything else. But it **seemed** as though I heard that. I tried to wake Cliff. **Perhaps** he was passed out. So I got up, **I think**, and went to the window. A big moon **appeared** to be laid over the mountains that **kind of** went around the city. It was **possibly** a white moon and **looked as though** it was covered with scars.

Depending on your changes, your negatively shaded version should make the narrator seem much less certain about the events in the story. The 'feel' is therefore much more mystery-like!

Practice question

In this advertisement, the car is the central image. A low-angle shot has been used to put the reader (following Kress and van Leeuwen) in a position of control with a suggestion that the product is within reach (despite the fact that Mercedes cars are notoriously expensive). The fact that this is a luxury car is shown in the way that it is presented: white, gleaming and standing out in light against a darker background of the margins and the rest of the advertisement. This provides connotations of a luxury product and enhances the product's 'buy in' factor. As with all advertisements, the image projects a lifestyle that would come with owning this product.

The noun phrase, 'Masterpiece of Intelligence' supports luxury branding, emphasising the high-spec nature of the car in a market where performance and extras are viewed as important ways of attracting potential buyers. However, the Mercedes-Benz brand on its own is also a strong influence and the advertisement relies on readers knowing about the reputation of the company and recognising its logo in the right-hand bottom corner. This means that very little other text is required, although the slogan 'The best or nothing' provides cohesion. Interestingly, the technical aspects of the car are in a smaller font and consequently downplayed to some degree, yet arguably still there to provide a more scientific basis for the claims being made about the car.

Chapter 3

Activity 3.3

The narrator's presentation of the beach becomes re-imagined as a narrative site. She offers a vivid description of the beach itself and the events that took place there, even including a backstory, 'it was so steep they had put railroad ties as stair steps', presumably to make the narrative more interesting for her listener. The narrator personalises and aligns her narrative through her own experience: she uses the first-person pronouns 'I' and 'we' in both narrative detail and evaluative comment, 'I'd say a couple of hundred yards', although her use of the generic second person 'you' at the beginning suggests that the beach was also more widely used and enjoyed by others. Equally, her recollections are framed by the use of 'this' as a determiner to pinpoint her memories and provide a richness of detail. The description she provides towards the end of her narrative offers a vivid image of the location, recalled through the act of narrating.

Practice question

Both speakers demonstrate a strong emotional connection to the place they are describing. Speaker A tends to lead the discussion with supporting comments from Speaker B, although this is clearly a jointly constructed narrative and the speakers are recounting a trip that they took together; consequently the memories themselves are shared ones.

The speakers use epistemic forms such as 'I thought' and 'I think' to outline their beliefs about Venice and to compare their initial mental model of Venice against what they discovered when they actually went there. They later draw on a range of places by name, for example 'St Mark's Square' and 'Palace Du Car', that evoke memories of their experiences and which have built up a richly defined sense of Venice.

The speakers work together by supporting each other and through agreed evaluations of Venice and their experiences there. Speaker B often agrees with Speaker A by using supportive responses such as 'yeah' and by upgrading her initial assessment, for example 'it was lovely' becomes 'it was really nice'. Later, the speakers upgrade each other's assessment when 'That was really good' (A) becomes 'That was really fantastic' (B), which in turn is further upgraded by 'That was brilliant' (A). Overall, the speakers work together to construct (or reconstruct) a mental version of Venice as a place that is richly reimagined, positively-oriented and shaped by their collective experiences there.

Chapter 4

Activity 4.1

The speaker initially orientates himself through the use of the deictic verbs 'leaving' and 'coming back'. Consequently, the reader is invited to share the space from which the events of the poem are viewed. Further deictic positioning is provided through the spatial adverb 'below', the prepositional phrase 'from 'the kitchen window' and the temporal markers 'all afternoon' and 'evening'.

In the fourth stanza, the switch to the present tense together with the deictic adverb 'there' initiates both temporal and spatial deictic shifts. This suggests some distance between this stanza and the narrated events of the first three, although the use of 'still' might be interpreted as the speaker struggling to completely disconnect himself from the events of the past. Again, the deictic verb 'return' orientates events towards the narrator and the temporal deixis 'then' and 'now' once more distinguishes between time frames but hints at a shared emotional connection. One interpretation is that the loss of the individual described in the poem is so strong that it persists across time, hence why the speaker is able to imagine himself across temporal zones still haunted by the memories.

Chapter 5

Activity 5.1

In this speech, Trump draws on the following metaphors:

- GEOGRAPHICAL AND POLITICAL ASSETS ARE OBJECTS: 'we must protect our borders', 'stealing our companies', 'destroying our jobs', 'we will bring back out wealth [...] our dreams'.

- **POLITICS IS WAR:** 'I will fight for you', 'America will start winning again'.

- **PROGRESS IS CONSTRUCTION:** 'We will build new roads, and highways, and bridges, and airports, and tunnels', 'We will get our people off of welfare and back to work – rebuilding our country'.

Trump appears to draw on source domains concerned with fighting back and reclaiming things that have been lost. These source domains cohere with the central messages of his campaign: America needs to be great again and what is now lost can be rediscovered and rebuilt under the Trump administration. This message promotes a particular view of a country (its borders, its economy and its infrastructure) that needs saving.

Activity 5.2

Zara is able to draw on her viewing of the film and shape her narrative in an interesting way. She begins with some description that sets the scene before adding specific narrative detail in the form of a complicating action, 'The snowman flies in the sky with the boy' and a resolution, 'At the end he melts'. Her evaluative point, 'The boy was sad' demonstrates an understanding of character and emotion. Overall, Zara presents her narrative in a logical and interesting way, is aware of how narrative sequences are structured, and shows a sense of writing for and entertaining a reader.

References

Abbott, H.P. (2008) *The Cambridge Introduction to Narrative* (Second Edition). New York, NY: Cambridge University Press.

Baker, P. (2014) *Using Corpora to Analyse Data*. London: Bloomsbury.

Bell, A. (1991) *The Language of the News Media*. Oxford: Blackwell.

Bourke, L. and Adams, A.M. (2010) 'Cognitive constraints and the early learning goals in writing', *Journal of Research in Reading* 33 (1), 94–110.

boyd, d. (2008) *Taken Out of Context: American Teen Sociality in Networked Publics*. Unpublished PhD Dissertation. University of California-Berkeley. Available at: www.danah.org/papers/

Charteris-Black, J. (2014) *Analysing Political Speeches: Rhetoric, Discourse and Metaphor*. Basingstoke: Palgrave Macmillan.

Clark, E.V. (2016) *First Language Acquisition* (Third edition). Cambridge: Cambridge University Press.

Crang, M. (1998) *Cultural Geography*. London: Routledge.

Everett, D. L. (2013) *Language: The Cultural Tool*. London: Profile Books.

Fowler, R. (1977) *Linguistics and the Novel*. London: Methuen.

Gee, J. P. (2015) *Social Linguistics and Literacies: Ideology in Discourses* (Fifth edition). New York, NY: Routledge.

Georgakopolou, A. (2007) *Small Stories: Interaction and Identities*. Amsterdam: John Benjamins.

Gerrig, R.J. (1993) *Experiencing Narrative Worlds: On the Psychological Activities of Reading*. New Haven, CT: Yale University Press.

Goffman, E. (1959) *The Presentation of Self in Everyday Life*. New York, NY: Anchor Books.

Goodwin, C. (1984) 'Notes on story structure and the organization of participation', in J. M. Atkinson and J. Heritage (eds) *Structures of Social Action: Studies in Conversation Analysis*. Cambridge: Cambridge University Press, pp. 225–246.

Heath, S.B. (1983) *Ways with Words: Language, Life And Work In Communities And Classrooms*. Cambridge: Cambridge University Press.

Kress, G. and van Leeuwen, T. (1996) *Reading Images: The Grammar of Visual Design*. Oxon: Routledge.

Labov, W. (1972) *Language in the Inner City: Studies in the Black English Vernacular*. Philadelphia, PA: University of Pennsylvania Press.

Lefèvre, P. (2011) 'Some Medium-Specific Qualities of Graphic Sequences', *SubStance* 40 (1): 14–33.

Mar, R. and Oatley, K. (2008) 'The function of fiction is the abstraction and simulation of social experience', *Perspectives on Psychological Science* 3 (3): 173–192.

Mason, J. (2014) 'Narrative' in P. Stockwell and S. Whiteley (eds) *The Cambridge Handbook of Stylistics*. Cambridge: Cambridge University Press, pp. 175–94.

McNeill, D. (2005) *Gesture and Thought*. Chicago, IL: University of Chicago Press.

Norrick, N.R. (2007) 'Conversational storytelling', in D. Herman (ed.) *The Cambridge Companion to Narrative*. Cambridge: Cambridge University Press, pp. 127–41.

Oatley, K. (1999) 'Why fiction may be twice as true as fact: Fiction as cognitive and emotional simulation', *Review of General Psychology* 3 (2): 101–117.

Ochs, E. and Capps, L. (2001) *Living Narrative: Creating Lives in Everyday Storytelling*. Cambridge, MA: Harvard University Press.

Olsen, G. (2003) 'Reconsidering unreliability: Fallible and untrustworthy narrators', *Narrative* 11 (1): 93–109.

Page, R. (2013) *Stories and Social Media: Identities and Interaction*. London: Routledge.

Pahl, K. (2007) 'Creativity in events and practices: a lens for understanding children's multimodal texts', *Literacy* 41 (2): 86–92.

Pomerantz, A. (1984) 'Agreeing and disagreeing with assessments: some features of preferred-dispreferred turn shapes', in J.M. Atkinson and J. Heritage (eds) *Structures of Social Action: Studies in Conversation Analysis*. Cambridge: Cambridge University Press, pp. 57–101.

Rothery, J. and Martin, J. (1980) *Writing Project Reports*. University of Sydney.

Sacks, H. (1984) 'On doing being ordinary', in J.M. Atkinson and J. Heritage (eds) *Structures of Social Action: Studies in Conversation Analysis*. Cambridge: Cambridge University Press, pp. 413–429.

Scollon, R. (1998) *Mediated Discourse as Social Interaction: A Study of News Discourse*. London: Longman.

Segal, E.M. (1995) 'Narrative comprehension and the role of deictic shift theory', in J.F. Duchan, G.A. Bruder and L.E. Hewitt (eds) *Deixis in Narrative: A Cognitive Science Perspective*. Hillsdale, NJ: Lawrence Erlbaum, pp. 3–17.

Semino, E. (1995) 'Deixis and the dynamics of poetic voice', in K. Green (ed.) *New Essays in Deixis: Discourse, Narrative, Literature*. Amsterdam: Rodopi, pp. 145–160.

Simpson, P. (1993) *Language, Ideology and Point of View*. London: Routledge.

Stockwell, P. (2009) *Texture: A Cognitive Aesthetics of Reading*. Edinburgh: Edinburgh University Press.

Tomasello, M. (2003) *Constructing a Language: A Usage-Based Theory of Language Acquisition*. Cambridge, MA: Harvard University Press.

Toolan, M. (2001) *Narrative: A Critical Linguistic Introduction* (Second edition). London: Routledge.

Wolf, M. (2007) *Proust and the Squid: The Science of the Reading Brain*. New York, NY: Harper Collins.

Glossary

active voice: the form where the agent is placed in the subject position in the clause for prominence

adjacency pair: a structure of two turns: a first pair part and second pair part

agent: the entity responsible for carrying out the verb in an action process

amplification strategy: a strategy that aims to ensure a user has a wider profile

assessment making: the act of evaluating something or someone when talking to others

asynchronous: communication where users do not post to each other in real time

avatar: an image-based representation of a user that accompanies a username

boulomaic modality: expressions that highlight aspects of desire

characterisation: the range of strategies authors and readers use to build, maintain and develop characters

collapsed contexts: the recognition that a user's online followers will be formed from different offline groups

conceptual metaphor: a structure that presents one concept in terms of another

constituent events: main events that are crucial to the direction of the story

critical discourse analysis: an approach to exploring texts that focuses on how power and ideologies are established and presented through language

defocus: the effect of drawing attention away from the agent through the use of the passive voice

deictic categories: types of deictic expressions (**person**, **spatial** and **temporal**)

deictic centre: the origin of an expression from which the expression points out and is understood

deictic shift: a movement between particular deictic fields, from one perceptual, temporal or spatial centre to another

deixis: words that are context-bound and whose meaning depends on who is using them, and where and when they are being used

deontic modality: expressions that highlight a sense of obligation or necessity

Discourse: a way of thinking and speaking about the world, informed by personal beliefs and group membership and ideologies

dispreferred response: a second part of an adjacency pair that doesn't fit in with what the speaker of the first part expects to hear

distal deixis: deictic expressions that refer to concepts, events or people at a distance from the speaker

downgrade: the lowering of the intensity of a speaker's assessment in a response to it

emergent writing: rudimentary writing that nonetheless shows evidence that a child understands that marks on a page communicate a message

epistemic modality: expressions that highlight degrees of belief, certainty or perception

exchange structure: sequence of turns between speakers

expert writer: a writer with developed technical awareness and skill

external evaluation: an expression of attitude towards the events where the speaker 'stands back' from the main action

external heterodiegetic narrative: a third-person narrative where the narrator is outside of the events of the story-world

face-threatening act: a speech act that has the potential to damage someone's self-esteem

fallible narrator: a narrator whose unreliability is a result of partial or limited knowledge

high tellability: a feature of a narrative whose events are interesting and which has a strong and identifiable purpose

homodiegetic narrative: a first-person narrative where the narrator is usually also a character in the story-world

ideal reader: the reader who agrees with the world-view projected in a text

implied author: the conceptual entity that a reader creates and has in mind when they read a particular piece of fiction

insertion sequence: an additional sequence between the two parts of an adjacency pair

intentionality: the belief that an author has a reason for shaping a narrative in a particular way

internal evaluation: an expression of attitude towards the events in a narrative that occur in the same time frame as the main action

internal heterodiegetic narrative: a third-person account where the narrator filters their account through the consciousness of a particular character

intertextuality: a process by which texts borrow from or refer to the content or conventions of other texts

literacy event: an occasion where an individual engages in a form of reading or writing

low tellability: a feature of a narrative whose events would be of little real interest to a listener

mind-modelling: the process by which readers construct and understand the mind of others

mind style: the distinctive way that a character's/narrator's mental self is shown through the language that they use

modal shading: the dominant type of modality in a text

modality: the term used to describe language that presents degrees of attitude or commitment

multimodal narrative: a narrative that draws on and combines different communicative modes

narratee: the person to whom a narrative is told

narrative: writing or speech that presents a series of events, characters and places in a coherent form

narrative discourse: the shaping and presentation of the story through choices in language and structure

narrative schema: an individual's mental version of a particular narrative

narrator: a person responsible for writing or speaking a narrative

novice writer: a writer with limited technical awareness and skill

objective narration: narration that is relatively free from any self-reference by the narrator

passive voice: the form where the agent is omitted or placed later in the clause

patient: the entity directly acted on by the verb in an action process

point of view: the perspective from which the narrative unfolds

preferred response: a second part of an adjacency pair that fits in with what the speaker of the first part expects to hear

proximal deixis: deictic expressions that refer to concepts, events or people close to the speaker

real author: the real-life human entity responsible for writing a piece of fiction

representation: the portrayal of events, people and circumstances through language and other meaning-making resources (e.g. images and sound) to create a way of seeing the world

schema: a bundle of information about something held in the mind

site of engagement: a social space in which groups of people come together to engage in a particular type of social practice

source domain: a domain of knowledge used to understand another concept (target domain)

story: the building blocks of a narrative in terms of events, entities, time and setting

subjective narration: narration where the narrator self-references so as to draw attention to themselves as much as the events of the narrative

supplementary events: secondary events that are not necessarily crucial to the overall story but are included and therefore foregrounded

synchronous: communication that takes place in real time and in a continuous exchange

target domain: the concept that is understood through another domain of knowledge (source domain)

tellability: the features of a story that make it worth telling to an audience

text-drivenness: the way that readers base their understanding on what is actually specified in the text

text–image cohesion: the way that text and images work together to create a sense of meaning

textual cue: a word or phrase that triggers a reader drawing on a schema

unreliable narrator: a narrator whose shaping of events is a distortion of actual events

untrustworthy narrator: a narrator whose unreliability is a result of some internal characteristic or strong emotional involvement that causes them to distort the truth

upgrade: the raising of the intensity of a speaker's assessment in a response to it

username: the online name assumed by a user

Index

Narrative

Acknowledgements

The authors and publishers acknowledge the following sources of copyright material and are grateful for the permissions granted. While every effort has been made, it has not always been possible to identify the sources of all the material used, or to trace all copyright holders. If any omissions are brought to our notice, we will be happy to include the appropriate acknowledgements on reprinting.

Text 1B Men's Health cover, by permission of Wright's Media; Text 1D from 'Leaver voters are not all idiots - some Londoners still don't get it' by Abi Wilkinson, The Guardian, February 2017 © Guardian News & Media 2017; Text 2I used by permission of Varde; Text 2L by permission of Daimler AG; Text 2M from BREAKS, Vieceli/Ryden, pub. Soaring Penguin Press 2017; Text 4C extract from "When You Go Away" by W. S. Merwin. Copyright © W. S. Merwin, 1993, used by permission of The Wylie Agency (UK) Limited and Copper Canyon Press; Text 5A from 'Liverpool libraries save after budget boost - for now' by Danuta Kean ' in The Guardian, March 2017, © Guardian News & Media 2017; Text 5B from The Times, © News Syndication; Text 5D from The Guardian © Guardian News & Media 2017; Data in Text 5K by permission of Rebecca Brown; Text 5V from The Sunday Herald

Development of this publication has made use of the Cambridge English Corpus (CEC). The CEC is a multi-billion word computer database of contemporary spoken and written English. It includes British English, American English and other varieties of English. It also includes the Cambridge Learner Corpus, developed in collaboration with Cambridge English Language Assessment. Cambridge University Press has built up the CEC to provide evidence about language use that helps to produce better language teaching materials.

Thanks to the following for permission to reproduce images:

Cover image Design Pics/Getty Images; Chapter 1 Image by Catherine MacBride/Getty Images; Fig. 1.1 Patrick Foto/Shutterstock; Fig. 1.3 FACUNDO ARRIZABALAGA/AFP/Getty Images; Fig. 1.4 Adina Tovy/Getty Images; Fig. 1.5 © Cavendish Press; Chapter 2 ~UserGI15633745/Getty Images; Fig. 2.2 Tatiana Bobkova/Shutterstock; Text 2J Jeremy Sutton-Hibbert/ Alamy Stock Photo; Text 2K Neil Baylis/Alamy Stock Photo; Chapter 3 Doug Armand/Getty Images; Chapter 4 Ulrike Schmitt-Hartmann/Getty Images; Chapter 5 Tara Moore/Getty Images

The publisher would like to thank the following members of The Cambridge Panel: English who assisted in reviewing this book: Peter Town, Obadia Somella, Angela Janovsky.